AMERICAN VOICES OF DISSENT

AMERICAN VOICES OF DISSENT

The Book from *XXI Century,*
a film by Gabriele Zamparini
and Lorenzo Meccoli

Routledge
Taylor & Francis Group

LONDON AND NEW YORK

First published 2005 by Paradigm Publishers

Published 2016 by Routledge
2 Park Square, Milton Park, Abingdon, Oxon OX14 4RN
711 Third Avenue, New York, NY 10017, USA

Routledge is an imprint of the Taylor & Francis Group, an informa business

Library of Congress Cataloging-in-Publication Data
American voices of dissent : The book from *XXI Century*, a film by Gabriele Zamparini and Lorenzo Meccoli.

p. cm.

ISBN 1-59451-133-0 (hc.)—ISBN 1-59451-134-9 (pbk.).

1. United States—Politics and government—2001– 2. United States—Military policy.
3. Presidents—United States—Election—2000. 4. September 11 Terrorist Attacks, 2001.
5. Civil rights—United States. 6. Journalism—Political aspects—United States. 7. Patriotism—
United States. 8. Petroleum industry and trade—Political aspects. 9. Iraq—Civilization. 10.
Dissenters—Interviews. I. Zamparini, Gabriele, 1968– II. Meccoli, Lorenzo, 1968– III. *XXI
Century.*

E902.A48 2005
973.931—dc22

2005008326

Designed and Typeset by Cheryl Hoffman

ISBN 13 : 978-1-59451-134-9 (pbk)

Contents

Foreword

William Blum

You are holding in your hands a book that would make an excellent time capsule; one to be opened, one would hope, in a future time when the United States was no longer on a rampage of imperial war and oppression around the world, no longer acting like a police state at home. This book captures the period of 2000 to 2003, from the highly questioned presidential election of 2000, to the infamous day of September 11, 2001, to the tearing up of the Bill of Rights by the Bush administration, to the historic 2002 and 2003 anti-war demonstrations determined to prevent the mad march to war in Iraq, to the onset of the war as Iraq was bombed and invaded.

Yet the period is more than this: Vietnam, the Gulf War, angry and disillusioned veterans of several wars of the American empire, their wounds and Gulf War syndrome eating away at them . . . Here's David Cline, the head of Veterans for Peace: "Well, war is when humans resort . . . descend to barbarism. It's when we go back to barbarism. And . . . and, in the end, war is men, and today, it's also women, but it's men going out there, from two different sides just trying to kill each other." Can it be put any simpler and more poignantly?

And in each of these wars, there was the routine use of depleted uranium and cluster bombs, two weapons designed by a mad scientist, which in a world not intimidated by the United States would be categorically banned.

Another horror as well: George W. Bush, calling on God to bless American warfare, mouthing one lie after another. And the prices we pay at home to support the military budget, equal to more than $20,000 per hour for every hour since Jesus Christ was born.

Many other bases are touched, including some intriguing history prior to this period about another empire, of the British variety, and its relation to Iraq, and Winston Churchill—the much revered Sir Winston—and his remarkable racism and use of poison gas. And the important previous history between the United States and Saddam Hussein is also included.

Crusading journalist Greg Palast speaks of the election in Florida in 2000, on which he is the leading expert, the election that put George W. into the White House, an election that illegally excluded about 90,000 people of color.

After the terrorist attack of 9/11, it was Christmas every day for the American national-security and corporate elite. All their wish lists were fulfilled, and then some. In short order, they massively increased the military budget; proposed sharp cutbacks of social spending; gave new life to the missile defense program; pushed through obscenely extensive tax breaks for the wealthy; launched efforts to cut back on environmental legislation; unilaterally abrogated a leading arms control treaty; extended the reach of the American empire under the rubric of an "anti-terrorism crusade"; created a new Office of Homeland Security; greatly increased surveillance and prosecutory powers over the American people, including license to enter their homes virtually at will; incarcerated over a thousand individuals for weeks or months, even years as it turned out, without charging them with a crime, and much more.

Much of these events are captured in the book, as in the film, by the people who questioned the official versions and the official lies, who protested in the streets, who fought in the courts and went to prison, who lost loved ones in the World Trade Center. "I don't want my husband's death to turn into the precipitating factor for more killing and more death," moans a widow. "Our grief is not a cry for war," shout the protesters.

"The Constitution, which protects our fundamental rights in the United States, is in great jeopardy," declares Michael Ratner, the courageous president of the Center for Constitutional Rights. "First, we have a clause of the Constitution called the 4th Amendment that protects the right to be free from government arrest without probable cause or without a reason. . . . The 4th Amendment, I would say, has basically been crossed out of the United States Constitution."

Gore Vidal speaks eloquently about the Constitution as well, and of much more. Noam Chomsky predicts how repressive governments around the world will use 9/11 to increase their repression; and so right he is.

Howard Zinn comments on the perverse idea of journalists being embedded with the military.

Various well-known progressive critics analyze how the corporate media has dealt with the events mentioned here; a selection of ultra-jingoist headlines from the American press captures the ugly mood.

Yes, it was, continues to be, an ugly time, but equally inspiring is the opposition to the ugliness, in the insistence that a better world is indeed possible.

NOTE

William Blum is the author of *Killing Hope: U.S. Military and CIA Interventions since World War II* and *Rogue State: A Guide to the World's Only Superpower.* Portions of these books can be accessed online at www.killinghope.org.

Acknowledgments

We would like to thank our publisher, Dean Birkenkamp, who believed in making a companion book to the documentary *XXI Century* and Dianne Ewing, Beth Davis, Melanie Stafford, and Alison Sullenberger of Paradigm Publishers for their help.

Just recently relocated to Europe, we lived in the United States for many years and learned to appreciate and love this beautiful country and its generous people. We learned things we didn't know and we met people we had no idea about. Making visible this America, which is too often neglected and ignored, both at home and abroad, is one of the main ideas behind this project.

We want to thank all the people who are featured in this work and hope their example will inspire many others to get involved and be active.

The documentary series *XXI Century* and this companion book *American Voices of Dissent* could never have been realized without the generosity of all the people who gave us their help, time, and work. The documentary credits are listed at the end of the book.

Who Is Who

Udi Aloni filmmaker and artist; interviewed on December 7, 2002

Jose Alvarez professor at Columbia Law School; interviewed on December 5, 2002

Asif (Ullah) member of War Resisters League; interviewed on January 23, 2003

Zainab Bahrani art historian at Columbia University; interviewed on March 26, 2003

Harry Belafonte actor and singer; speaking at the February 15, 2003, anti-war demonstration, New York City

Phyllis Bennis member of Institute for Policy Studies; speaking at the February 15, 2003, anti-war demonstration, New York City

Darril Bodley member of September Eleventh Families for Peaceful Tomorrows; speaking at the February 15, 2003, anti-war demonstration, New York City

Julian Bond chairman of the National Association for the Advancement of Colored People (NAACP) board of directors; speaking at the February 15, 2003, anti-war demonstration, New York City

Reed Brody advocacy director of Human Rights Watch; interviewed on December 3, 2002

Leslie Cagan political analyst at Pacifica Foundation, national coordinator of United for Peace and Justice; interviewed on November 26, 2002, and speaking at the February 15, 2003, anti-war demonstration, New York City

Noam Chomsky political analyst; linguist at Massachusetts Institute of Technology; interviewed on February 21, 2003

Ramsey Clark former US attorney general; speaking at the House of the Lord Church, Brooklyn, New York, November 21, 2002

David Cline   president of Veterans for Peace; interviewed on February 3, 2003

Rachel Coen   political analyst at Fairness and Accuracy in Reporting (FAIR); interviewed on December 9, 2002

Edward Daniels II   member of Incarcerated Veteran Consortium; interviewed on February 16, 2003

Angela Davis   political activist; professor at University of California–Santa Cruz; speaking at the February 15, 2003, anti-war demonstration, New York City

Ossie Davis   actor; speaking at the February 15, 2003, anti-war demonstration, New York City

Victoria De Grazia   historian at Columbia University; interviewed on April 6, 2003, and on May 11, 2003

Beverly Eckert   member of September Eleventh Families for Peaceful Tomorrows; interviewed on March 5, 2003

Ken Estey   Member of Peace Action; interviewed on November 15, 2002

Liza Featherstone   columnist at *The Nation;* interviewed on November 13, 2002

Michael Foley   historian at City University of New York's College of Staten Island; interviewed on February 26, 2003

Cheshire Frager   (at the time of the interview) member of American Friends Service Committee (The Quakers); winner of Nobel Peace Prize (1947); interviewed on December 4, 2002

Danny Glover   actor; speaking at the February 15, 2003, anti-war demonstration, New York City

Curt Goering   senior deputy executive director of Amnesty International USA; winner of Nobel Peace Prize (1977); interviewed on May 15, 2003

Amy Goodman   host and executive producer of *Democracy Now!* interviewed on November 23, 2002, and speaking at the West Park Presbyterian Church, December 1, 2002, New York City

William Hartung   President's Fellow of World Policy Institute; interviewed on May 1, 2003

Larry Holmes   co-director of International A.N.S.W.E.R.; speaking at the House of the Lord Church, Brooklyn, New York, November 21, 2002

Rev. Jesse Jackson   founder of Rainbow–PUSH Coalition; speaking at the October 26, 2003, and January 18, 2003, anti-war demonstrations, Washington, DC

Leslie Kauffman   member of United for Peace and Justice; interviewed on February 7, 2003

Martin Luther King III   member of Southern Christian Leadership Conference; speaking at the February 15, 2003, anti-war demonstration, New York City

Molly Klopot   member of Not In Our Name (NION); member of Women's International League for Peace and Freedom; interviewed on January 23, 2003

Rev. Peter Laarman   reverend at Judson Memorial Church in New York; member of New York Forum of Concerned Religious Leaders; interviewed on November 14, 2002

Anna Landau   member of Columbia University Anti-War Coalition; interviewed on October 21, 2002, and on October 26, 2002

Jessica Lange   actor; speaking at the January 18, 2003, anti-war demonstration, Washington, DC

Donna Lieberman   executive director of New York Civil Liberties Union; interviewed on February 18, 2003, and speaking at the February 15, 2003, anti-war demonstration, New York City

Valerie Lucznicowfka   member of September Eleventh Families for Peaceful Tomorrows; interviewed on February 14, 2003

Nelson Mandela   former South Africa president; winner of Nobel Peace Prize (1993); speaking at the International Women's Forum, Johannesburg, South Africa, January 30, 2003

Amit Mashiah   member of Courage to Refuse; speaking at the February 15, 2003, anti-war demonstration, New York City

Arno J. Mayer   historian at Princeton University; interviewed on February 19, 2003

Hanny Megally   (at the time of the interview) member of Human Rights Watch; interviewed on December 3, 2002

Timothy Mitchell   professor of Middle Eastern Studies at New York University and at Hagop Kevorkian Center for Near Eastern Studies; interviewed on December 12, 2002

Tony Murphy   member of International A.N.S.W.E.R.; interviewed on November 12, 2002

Roger Normand   (at the time of the interview) political analyst at Center for Economic and Social Rights; interviewed on March 19, 2003

Rosemarie Pace   member of Pax Christi; interviewed on December 11, 2002

Greg Palast   investigative reporter at BBC and *The Guardian;* interviewed on March 9, 2003

William Perkins   deputy majority leader of New York City Council; interviewed on March 18, 2003

Katha Pollitt   columnist at *The Nation*; interviewed on February 26, 2003

Sister Elizabeth Proefriedt   member of Pax Christi; interviewed on December 11, 2002

Michael Ratner   president of Center for Constitutional Rights; interviewed on January 29, 2003

Emily Reinhardt   writer at Indymedia; interviewed on January 24, 2003

Scott Ritter   former United Nations weapons inspector; interviewed on February 15, 2003

Clayton Roberts   (Florida director of Election 2000); interviewed by Greg Palast in 2000

Tim Robbins   actor; speaking at the October 6, 2002, anti-war demonstration, New York City

Susan Sarandon   actor; speaking at the October 6, 2002, and February 15, 2003, anti-war demonstrations, New York City

Danny Schechter   journalist and filmmaker; founder and executive editor of MediaChannel.org; founder, vice president, and executive producer of Globalvision Inc.; interviewed on March 13, 2003

Dread Scott   artist; interviewed on February 4, 2003

Pete Seeger   singer and songwriter; interviewed on April 11, 2003

Rev. Al Sharpton   co-founder of National Action Network; speaking on December 8, 2002, at the Riverside Church, New York City; at the January 18, 2003, anti-war demonstration, Washington DC; and at the February 15, 2003, anti-war demonstration, New York City

Victor Sidel   former co-president of International Physicians for the Prevention of Nuclear War (IPPNW); winner of Nobel Peace Prize (1985); interviewed on February 25, 2003

Norman Solomon   founder and executive director of Institute for Public Accuracy; interviewed on April 1, 2003

Jacqueline Soohen   journalist, media activist, and filmmaker; interviewed on April 12, 2003

Monica Tarazi   member of American-Arab Anti-Discrimination Committee; interviewed on February 5, 2003

Setsuko Nakamura Thurlow   Hiroshima survivor; speaking at the West Park Presbyterian Church, December 1, 2002, New York City

Archbishop Desmond Tutu   winner of Nobel Peace Prize (1984); speaking at the February 15, 2003, anti-war demonstration, New York City

Gore Vidal   writer and historian; interviewed by Amy Goodman in May 2003, and also giving a speech organized by the Nation Institute on May 4, 2003, New York City

Laura Vild   member of Not In Our Name (NION); interviewed on January 23, 2003

Edmund White   writer; interviewed on February 10, 2003

Julia Willebrand   member of Green Party; interviewed on January 26, 2003

Howard Zinn   historian at Boston University; interviewed on March 4, 2003

Introduction

I love America more than any other country in the world, and, exactly
for this reason, I insist on the right to criticize her perpetually.
—James Baldwin, *Notes of a Native Son*

Since September 11, 2001, Americans have lined up after the president, a new reinvigorated and spontaneous patriotism have united the country, and the flag has returned to be the symbol of the American values. The corporate media have sold the story. TV channels, radio stations, and newspapers have explained to us what America is, what America feels, what America thinks. If you've happened to be, to feel, to think something else, your problem! You must be crazy, un-American, unpatriotic. Or just too stupid to understand. You'd rather not speak out your mind.

American Voices of Dissent tells a different story. From September 2002 to May 2003 we met with journalists, university professors, writers, artists, historians, political analysts, international observers, human and civil rights fighters, students, religious leaders, Vietnam War veterans, peace and anti war activists, demonstrators, and ordinary Americans, asking questions to understand and try to put together the many pieces of a complicated puzzle.

The 2000 presidential elections and September 11, 2001. Afghanistan, Iraq, terrorism, and weapons of mass destruction. The first Gulf War and the UN sanctions against Iraq. Saddam Hussein and the inspections. The axis of evil, the coalition of the willing, and collateral damage. News, media, concentrations of power, and censorship. The Middle East and the old and new colonialism. The Constitution, the Bill of Rights, civil liberties, and human rights. United Nations, International

1

Criminal Court, and the Old Europe. War, peace, and patriotism. The anti-war movement, oil, blood, and the voices of dissent. Is it possible to find interconnecting links?

We wanted to tell the story of the American anti-war movement from the voices of its protagonists. The result was far beyond our expectations. The picture that comes alive is—to paraphrase James Baldwin—"longer, larger, more various, more beautiful, and more terrible than anything anyone has ever said about it."

In times of danger and madness, voices of reason are voices of dissent.

American Voices of Dissent tells the story of this America, people you don't see in the corporate media. It's not just a book. It's a call to join millions of brothers and sisters in the United States, millions of brothers and sisters all over the world.

On February 15, 2003, more than 35 million people demonstrated all over the world. They took over the streets of the planet to oppose the Bush administration's imminent war of aggression against Iraq. Thirty-five million people from different nationalities, different ethnicities, different religions, different languages, united by the will to live in a better world. United to build justice, freedom, democracy, and peace. This book is dedicated to them and to the many more to come!

Gabriele Zamparini
Lorenzo Meccoli
May 2005

Union Square, New York City, September 15, 2001

Anti-war demonstration in Central Park, New York City, October 6, 2002

"The Dawn": Election 2000 and Its Aftermath

And that government of the people, by the people, for the people shall not perish from the earth.
—Abraham Lincoln, 16th US president (1861–1865)

GEORGE W. BUSH (taking the oath on January 20, 2001): I, George Walker Bush, do solemnly swear that I will faithfully execute the office of president of the United States.

GREG PALAST: Bush has taken control of the White House through an election that was basically an apartheid election. . . . [There's] George Bush's brother, Jeb, who is the governor of Florida, and [there's] the secretary of state of Florida who's in charge of voting, who happened to also be the chairwoman of his presidential campaign, Katherine Harris. So you have his campaign chief, [and] . . . his brother as the governor, running the election. And they took advantage of it.

AMY GOODMAN: Jeb Bush and Katharine Harris, secretary of state, made a deal with a private company, spent 4 million dollars, gave it to DBT [Database Technologies] to purge the voter rolls. . . .

Greg Palast interviews Clayton Roberts, Florida director of Election 2000 (from the documentary Counting on Democracy *by Danny Schechter).*

CLAYTON ROBERTS: We have a statute that says we have to have a private company to do this. We put it out for a bid, they [DBT] got the bid, and I think I am done with this interview.

GREG PALAST: Wait, let me just show you the contract if I could. . . . Mr. Roberts . . . Look, Mr. Roberts, I am not trying to give you a tough time. . . . Mr. Roberts . . .

Clayton Roberts takes off his microphone and walks out of the room.

GREG PALAST: They made up a list of 94,000 people and they removed them from the voting rolls of Florida. They said that "they can't vote." The reason they said they can't vote is, they said, "They're all criminals." And in Florida, if you're a convicted criminal you lose your right to vote. In fact, almost none of them were convicted criminals. Of the 94,000, 91,000 at least were completely innocent of any crime except that over half of them were guilty of being black or Hispanic.

Greg Palast interviews an African American man whose name was purged from the voters list (from Counting on Democracy *by Danny Schechter).*

MAN: I have never spent a night in jail. Never have. . . .

GREG PALAST: You were never busted?

MAN: No, I [had] a speeding ticket probably twenty-five, thirty years ago I guess, something like that, but that's about it.

GREG PALAST: You think you should be allowed to vote if you had a speeding ticket?

MAN: Absolutely . . . absolutely.

GREG PALAST: And almost all those voters vote Democratic. And you have to understand that in the state of Florida, the entire presidency of the United States was determined in the state of Florida by 537 votes. That's it; 537 votes. Then we moved on to the Supreme Court in America, which was basically fixed. In fact, the members who voted to give George Bush the election, one of them actually said, "We better stop the vote count in Florida." So, the Supreme Court stopped it. It was a completely political decision by people put in by his father and his political allies.

AMY GOODMAN: So maybe it's best rather than saying President Bush, Resident Bush. . . .

Although we may never know with complete certainty the identity of the winner of this year's presidential election, the identity of the loser is perfectly clear. It is the nation's confidence in the judge as an impartial guardian of the rule of law.

—Justice John Paul Stevens,
United States Supreme Court, December 2000

GREG PALAST: Even Al Gore, who lost the race through theft, he's so ingrained in the system. He's a very rich kid. He was a senator. He's a part of the power structure. He was more concerned about saving the image and authority of the power structure than he was about getting the votes counted.

DANNY SCHECHTER: After the election I felt it was time to go back and have a second look, to investigate what happened in Florida. And the idea was to try to speak to the voters and analyze what actually happened, how the recount was sabotaged and why the Democrats also didn't educate voters enough. They registered them but they didn't educate them. So this is an indictment, really, of the political system, of both political parties and of the American media, which failed to do a good job. There were 350 news crews in Palm Beach, Florida. But they missed the big story. They did not really understand what was actually happening to the voters of Florida. As we all know, the television news media in America called the election prematurely. They called Bush as a winner when in fact the election was too close to call when all the votes had not yet been counted. That might have affected the election itself.

DAN RATHER (from the CBS News program, the night of the elections): Texas Governor George Bush is elected the 43rd president of the United States. . . . The CBS News has now, for the second time tonight, pulled back Florida. . . .

DANNY SCHECHTER: But beyond that they failed to really investigate— how voters in Florida were disenfranchised. They didn't really report on the way in which the people who had been in prison were disqualified from voting, [disqualified] often improperly. They didn't really report on the racial bias of the exclusion of voters. They didn't really report on the problems of the butterfly ballot. In other words, there was no background offered. There was no attempt to really ensure that all votes were counted and that's really the essence of democracy: count every vote. And all votes weren't counted. And as a consequence, the man that won the national majority, Al Gore, lost the election because of Florida's electoral votes and because of the intervention of the United States Supreme Court. Parts of the story were told, but a lot of the story was not told. And that's why we made the film *Counting on Democracy.*

RACHEL COEN: I think what I took out of it, more powerfully than any impression, was realizing how committed much of the media, the mainstream press, is—not to the left or the right, but simply to the status quo and to a certain type of stability.

GREG PALAST: The story of the wipeout of the black voters was reported in Europe. I uncovered the story. I reported it for BBC Television. I reported it in the Guardian Observer newspapers, and I couldn't report it in the United States. The editors here did not want to hear anything but how wonderful our election system is and how democratic.

KATHA POLLITT: But, it felt as if they had all said, "Okay, he's the president and our job is to accept that and the story is over, we're not going to go back over that ground."

RACHEL COEN: We saw lots of commentary saying "time to move on, time to move on."

I remember the *New York Times* ran a front-page news analysis piece by R. W. Apple explaining that this whole upset election might seem discomforting right now, but after the Americans had gotten used to seeing George W. Bush looking presidential on TV newscasts they would come to accept the idea.

GEORGE W. BUSH (addressing the nation in a televised speech, November 26, 2000): Tonight after a count, a recount, and yet another manual recount, Secretary Cheney and I are honored and humbled to have won the State of Florida, which gives us the needed electoral votes to win the election.

> *A bad beginning makes a bad ending.*
> —Euripides, *Aeolus*

GREG PALAST: So now we have a guy in the White House who's talking about bringing democracy to Iraq, yet we have a guy who made sure there was no democracy in Florida.

HOWARD ZINN: Bush received not the majority of the popular vote. Al Gore, his opponent, received the majority of the popular vote, and Bush was put into the office by 5 to 4 votes by the Supreme Court. It was a coup you might say, really; not an election, a coup.

GORE VIDAL: Well, the election of 2000 was the end of the republic. This is corporate America, as one, putting in place a president who was not elected, getting the Supreme Court to delay and delay. When under the 10th Amendment, every decision about the voting in Florida should be made by the Florida Supreme Court, not the US Supreme Court, which the Constitution rules out in matters of election. And it was stolen by the secretary of state—that lady who has now been rewarded with a seat in Congress. The president's brother; the losing president candidate's brother, was governor and he took part in it. And, the Court did, by 5 to 4. Two of the five should've recused themselves; should've just withdrawn from the case when Gore vs. Bush came before the Court. Why? One of them; Scalia, had a son who was working for the Bush team of lawyers before the Supreme Court. Does Justice Scalia recuse himself, as he should because his son is arguing? No, he wants to kill Gore. He wants to make sure that the bad guys win. [Clarence] Thomas's wife was busy getting curricula vitae of potential people to serve in a Bush administration. . . . Thomas should have recused himself and withdrawn from the case. In which case, it would've been 4 to 3 for Gore, who would now be president, and Iraq and Afghanistan, I can guarantee, would not have been knocked down in order to benefit Halliburton and Bechtel.

And back of that, there's [an] interesting organization going on which is hard to determine—Opus Dei. Both Scalia and Thomas have connections with Opus Dei, which is a secret Catholic order; originally Fascist. General Franco in Spain was a sort of godfather to it. And, we don't know much about it. I make no charges but I simply bring up questions. Why not ask questions [of] these people? Does it suit Opus Dei that Bush is president? Now we're getting into God territory, which I normally would stay away from, as any good American should. It's not my business, other people's religions. But, Bush is born-again. That's why he uses biblical language. "He's evil . . . he's evil. He's an evil-doer." Well, that's theological language. He didn't say he's a bad man. He didn't say he's a dishonest man, ruthless man . . . [he said] "evil-doer"! And, he believes the end of the world is coming. Born-agains believe in rapture. They don't care about this world. When it ends, he's going to be lifted up; George W. Bush will be lifted up into a state of rapture, into the bosom of our Lord. Also, among the born-again category, though not that kind of Protestant, is Tony Blair, who has become, like his wife, Roman Catholic. So, now we have two boys who think that Jesus wants them for sunbeams, who are willing to put at risk. . . . I'm extrapolating on my own just from the evidence at hand. This is mostly humorous. You can judge it as you may. But two believers in our Lord's coming, an Armageddon, and the end of the world; that's the way Ronald Reagan used to talk and made him very popular in the Southern states. Those states don't have much in the way of population. But they have very strong born-again evangelical Christians, Protestants, and they believe in our Lord returning at any moment. They are the swing vote in those states because of the Electoral College. They don't have much population but they have a lot of electoral votes among them. The Electoral College was devised . . . you call yourself a democracy. You're very un-American. The founding fathers did not want democracy in the United States, ever. They also did not want tyranny—a king or a Hitler. They wanted a Republic. And they devised the Electoral College so the majority could never control anything. So, you have a popular vote out there, and those days they were just for Congress. Then there was one electoral vote per congressman, one per senator in the state and some other officials. And they get together and decide the election. So, what Scalia was doing is he was going back to the Electoral College in order to put together a majority to put in his candidate who will probably hasten the end of the world. I don't know where Scalia will be during rapture. . . .

> *Either you are with us, or you are with the terrorists.*
> —George W. Bush, 43rd US president

VALERIE LUCZNICOWFKA: I got to the corner of 18th Street and there was a street-side vendor there with his cart and he had his car door open and he was listening to the radio and I stood and I listened to the reports and I couldn't believe what I was hearing. But, just then, one of the buildings fell and I'm not sure which building it was at that point, but I was completely stunned as everyone was and I walked slowly down 18th Street and suddenly, I looked over and there was a young man, oh, I would say, in his late 30s, standing in the middle of the street (luckily, there were no cars coming) and he was crying hysterically and I walked over to him and I put my arm around him and I said, "Did you lose someone?" And he said, "No, but it's so terrible." And, I took him and I led him over and I kind of put him next to a car where he was safe, never for a moment thinking that I might have lost someone. It never occurred to me and I walked on. And, as I came to the doctor's office, I realized that my nephew worked in the second World Trade [Center] tower, on the 84th floor.

My nephew's body was found the next week. He had gotten out of the building but was crushed by the building when it fell. He was found not far from the building.

BEVERLY ECKERT: My husband had taken an early train to work. If he had taken a later train, he wouldn't have been there. We spoke on the phone actually. He called my office about 8 a.m. We were making plans for the weekend. We were actually going to stay in the hotel that's connected to the World Trade Center. We were going to come back on the weekend and spend the weekend in New York. We were together since we were 16 years old. We met very early and he was the only person for me for thirty-four years. . . . The morning of September 11, we both went to work and I was in a meeting and I heard that a plane had hit the World Trade Center, so I ran to my phone, I had a message from him saying it was the other building. As soon as I heard the second building was hit, I wanted as much information as I could. I left a message on my answering machine, "Sean, I'm home, I went home." I heard from him at 9:30, at which point I was like, "Sean, where are you?" thinking he's going to tell me he's on Broadway or something and he said, "I'm on the 105th floor." That's when I knew he wasn't coming home. When we realized that, and the smoke was filling the area where he was, we took the opportunity to say good-bye. I was able to tell him how much I loved him and that he'd made me very happy.

VALERIE LUCZNICOWFKA: A particularly disturbing thing is that my government is using the events of 9/11 and the names of those who died for [the] purposes of gaining territory that's filled with oil.

BEVERLY ECKERT: I don't want my husband's death to turn into the precipitating factor for more killing and more death.

WILLIAM PERKINS: As one who lost a cousin in that terrorist attack on September 11th, I and many other New Yorkers are very concerned about fighting terrorism. And it was important to us to say to our president and the world . . . that our fight for terrorism is not an opportunity to declare war in our name.

DREAD SCOTT: One of the more significant works that I did was also a collaborative work called "Our Grief Is Not a Cry for War," which was a public performance that happened shortly after September 11th. It was first performed on September 22nd, where 100 artists stood, all wearing black, all wearing dust masks, which became sort of the symbol of New York because the air was so putrid from the burning towers and all wearing signs that said, "Our Grief Is Not a Cry for War" and we stood silently for one hour with our hands on each other's shoulders.

REV. PETER LAARMAN: We did a program on the second day after the attack where we said "grief, anger, and what else are we feeling" because it was clear that Bush was going to use this tragedy and turn it into an occasion to save his presidency by militarizing the whole culture.

BEVERLY ECKERT: I understand the reaction that people have when [we] are wounded, when [we] are threatened; we don't always react with objectivity. But I understood from the way I was controlling those reactions that it could be done. And, I was hoping to find other family members who would join me in this voice for . . . dialogue.

VALERIE LUCZNICOWFKA: I did not hear of "Peaceful Tomorrows" until very recently. I had gone to Senator Schumer's office last fall to protest the resolution that was before the Senate to give the president the right to declare war without going to Congress. And, I had no signs, so I took the only thing that I found handy before I left, which was the poster of my nephew giving his description and I wrote at the bottom of it, "Not in his name."

SUSAN SARANDON (speaking at the February 15, 2003, anti-war demonstration in New York City): I am so very moved to be able to introduce Darril Bodley to you. Darril Bodley lost his only child, Deora Bodley, on September 11th, 2001, at the World Trade Center.

DARRIL BODLEY (speaking at the February 15, 2003, anti-war demonstration in New York City): Mr. President, I urge you to listen to the world leaders who are strongly advising against going down the path of war. We, the September Eleventh Families for Peaceful Tomorrows, traveling to Iraq last month and Afghanistan last year, we saw the graves of the victims of violence there, victims of interminable wars, bombing, and brutality. We, who on September 11th lost a brother, a daughter, a sister, a mother, we met our own twins in Iraq and Afghanistan, persons there who lost a loved one just like ours, just as much loved as ours, just as human as we are. Their grief is our grief. Their pain, their fears, and their hopes are the same as our own. Shall we continue the death, destruction, and disease that [have] already been heaped upon Iraq? We say no. Not in our names, not in our loved ones' names.

BEVERLY ECKERT: A group of family members was dedicated to ensuring that an independent commission was created. We began our activism, trying to get that established by visiting Washington, by holding a rally, writing letters, going to the media. . . . a number of different ways. We met

Valerie Lucznicowfka and Beverly Eckert of September 11 Families for Peaceful Tomorrows at the anti-war demonstration in New York, February 15, 2003

with incredible resistance. When we finally achieved the goal of legislation creating a commission, I want to say, we were not celebrating—we were wearied, we were disillusioned. So we went to the signing. Some of the family members who were instrumental in getting that bill passed wouldn't even attend. That's how strongly we felt about how the White House had changed it and diminished the ability of the commission. So, we went to the signing and President Bush came out to the podium and he was followed by Henry Kissinger. We did not know that the appointment of the commissioner was going to be announced at the same time as the bill signing. So, I said to the family member next to me, "Is that Henry Kissinger?" And he said, "Yes." And I said, "Well, what is he doing here?" And Steve answered me and said, "He must be . . . Bush must be appointing him today—Henry Kissinger." And I said . . . my reaction was, "Isn't he a war criminal?"

GEORGE W. BUSH (signing the 9/11 Commission bill, White House, November 27, 2002): Today I am pleased to announce my choice for commission chairman, Doctor Henry Kissinger. Doctor Kissinger is one of our nation's most accomplished and respected public servants. He worked here at the White House as a national security advisor. Representing America abroad as a secretary of state for two presidents. He is a distinguished author, academic, army veteran, and winner of the Nobel Peace Prize.

REED BRODY: Henry Kissinger was the architect of American policies that resulted in incredible human suffering in countries like Chile, Vietnam, Cambodia, Laos, East Timor. . . . It's the very policy of imperial America that Henry Kissinger implemented that has created such resentment against the United States and provided fertile ground for the worst kind of terrorist activities.

BEVERLY ECKERT: Luckily, it wasn't just the families who recognized that. There was an [upsurge] of world opinion and, certainly, in the United States, against that appointment, and now Kissinger has been replaced by Governor Tom Keane. But I do want to say that that commission has been absolutely stalled. They have not gotten security clearance for the commissioners on their staff yet, they haven't been given access to classified documents, and I believe those stall tactics are continuing. This frightens me. It should frighten all Americans.

THE MOST CENSORED STORY IN AMERICA

GREG PALAST: Okay . . . first of all, we have to start out with this. A lot of people think that George Bush planned or knew about the September 11th attack in advance. There's no evidence of that at all. I want to get that clarified right away. First of all, my idea that George Bush knows about anything at all, you better prove it to me . . . you know, the idea that he's capable of having this huge brilliant scheme to increase his own authority is very unlikely. But here's what BBC Television did find out. I was able to report again in Europe but not here . . . that Bush had put limits on investigations by our intelligence agencies on investigating the money behind the terrorists before September 11th; because Saudi Arabia is the source of almost all the funding. And you could not touch the guys that were giving the money to make Al-Qaeda operate. Now a lot of this, we believe, was determined in a meeting in Paris in 1996. The Cobar Towers were attacked within Saudi Arabia. Nineteen American military people were killed while they were sleeping. That was Al-Qaeda. The Saudis, rather than go after these guys and capture them, basically went to them and said "How much does it cost" for you to go play in Afghanistan instead or Uzbekistan? And by the way, it's not just paying them protection money to get lost; they actually wanted Al-Qaeda to spread the word of wahabism and sell to Central Asian republics, the kind of vicious, small-minded, feudal state that they have in Saudi Arabia. Of course, the Al-Qaeda's vision was that it's not feudal enough and it's not terrible enough. You know, don't forget, just wanted to remind you; people forget this often in Europe. The guys who attacked America, [they] didn't attack America because we are the center of globalization and powerful capitalist expansion. These guys do not represent the wretched of the earth. These guys are Saudi billionaires. But Bush did not want any investigation of the guys behind Al-Qaeda until after September 11th.

I even have the documents from the FBI, secret documents that were dropped off by FBI agents to me and my team at BBC, which said that the investigation of the bin Laden family which had been stopped was reopened on September 13th of 2001, two days after the attack. In other words, before the attack you couldn't touch the American side of the bin Laden family. Why? Because there's this long financial, political relationship between the bin Ladens and the Bushes, except for Osama. Osama, we've always been hunting because he's a complete maniac. However, the rest of the family, which is connected to the Bush family financially and connected of course to the Saudi Arabian royals, they're off limits to investigation. And it was very important that they'd be investigated because these guys, the organization they were fronting in the United States called WAMY, World Assembly of Muslim Youth . . . some of it's very nice activity they do. But a lot of their people are involved in recruiting Jihadis and recruiting people for . . . they were promoting . . . I saw tapes that they made promoting hostage-takings, promoting suicide bombing, promoting murder of civilians, and attacks worldwide. I mean, these are not nice guys and one of their people was in fact the conduit for an Osama bin Laden audiotape. So, these are the guys that probably should've been investigated. They really are dangerous. But why weren't they? Because it would upset the Saudi Arabians, and we broke that story. You couldn't get that story in the United States for anything. We won a . . . the BBC and *The Guardian* paper won a . . . California State University award, a journalism school award for The Most Censored Story in America. This is played all over the world. In fact, I just talked to Noam Chomsky a few days ago and he was saying that he read the story in the front page of the *Times of India* and was wondering why wasn't it in the US. And I said, "Noam, what do you mean why wasn't it in the US, you've written the book, you know, *Manufacturing Consent*." They can't allow this information into the US because it takes away George Bush as the great hero and starts putting up the idea of the Bush family as being connected to the people funding the terrorists. Again, not that Bush planned the attack, but the question is, How much protection is there of the people behind the attackers? That's a very serious question which is not being addressed before the American public.

They also wanted to investigate why there were investigation failures. Why didn't our FBI . . . we paid a trillion dollars to our intelligence agencies over the past few decades. I mean, a trillion dollars; we're talking big, big, big money. And yet we didn't see this coming, Why? They don't want to ask that. And again, it's not because Bush planned it, but because if you ask why we weren't looking, you end up going back to a few names that ought to be investigated. I don't know all the things that they've done, but investigations say we've got to be looking at Sheikh Abdullah Bakhsh, Adnan Khashoggi, and others who may be involved in funding terrorism worldwide. And not necessarily willingly, but money goes to charities that they fund, which end up in the wrong hands. Now, who's Sheikh Abdullah Bakhsh? He's the guy who saved Harken Oil in the 1980s from bankruptcy. Harken Oil is George W. Bush's oil company. So, you've got the guy who funds the president's oil company, maybe a guy whose money ended up in the hands of the people killing us. Why isn't there an investigation? Congressmen wanted to know. One congresswoman, Cynthia McKinney, asked, "Why aren't we investigating these guys?" and they destroyed her political career. The *Times* actually wrote that she said that George Bush knew about the attack in advance and didn't tell anyone so his business partners would make money. The quote's a complete, absolute fabrication, a lie. It's completely out of the air. This congresswoman, Cynthia McKinney, never ever said it, ever. And when I challenged the *New York Times* on it, I challenged them on it. I said, "What's the source?" They couldn't find it. They told me, "Oh, it was in the congressional record. It wasn't there." In other words, they fabricated; they literally fabricated the quote.

We were able to locate a diplomat, a foreign American diplomat, who was in Saudi Arabia. And he said he was issuing visas at the demand of the US State Department to people who clearly were involved in terrorist activities. But it was terrorism that we liked. It was Osama bin Laden's gang who were the precursor groups, the Jihadi groups, who were recruited by the US, the CIA, and State Department. [They were] being given false visas, which Springman was forced to issue out of Saudi Arabia. [Bin Laden's gang was] sent to the United States for training to go fight in Afghanistan. So, we were more than happy to let these people fight in Afghanistan. We were kind of happy. We encouraged them. We even armed them and gave them money to fight in Afghanistan. The point of

Springman was that he was taking us back to the origin of these terrorists. How did they get so sophisticated? How did they learn to fly planes? How did they learn this logistical information? How did they learn how to set up networks and to work clandestinely? The answer is that they were trained by the United States. And it blew up in our face. It's called "blow-back" in the intelligence community. It happens, OK, and there should be an honest discussion in America.

PERPETUAL WAR FOR PERPETUAL PEACE

GORE VIDAL: The United States is not a normal country. We are under . . . we are a homeland now, under military surveillance and military control. The president asked the Congress right after 9/11 not to conduct a major investigation as it might deter our search for terrorism wherever it may be in the world. So, Congress obediently rolled over. . . . I remember Pearl Harbor. I was a kid then, and within three years of it I enlisted in the Army. That's what we did in those days. We did not go off to the Texas Air Force and hide. I realize the country has totally changed, that the government is not responsive to the people either in protecting us from something like 9/11, which they should've done, could've done, did not do. And then when it did happen, to investigate, investigate, investigate. So, I wrote two little books. One called *Perpetual War for Perpetual Peace*, in which I try to go into why Osama bin Laden, if it were he or whoever it was—why it was done. Then I wrote another one, *Dreaming War*, on why we were not protected at 9/11, which ordinarily would've led to the impeachment of the president of the United States, would allow it to happen. They said they had no information. Since then, every day the *New York Times* prints another mountain of people who said they had warned the government, they had warned the government. President Putin of Russia; he had warned us. President Mubarak of Egypt; he had warned us. Three members of Mossad claimed that they had come to the United States to warn us that some time in September something unpleasant might come out of the sky in our direction. Were we defended? No, we were not defended. Has this ever been investigated? No, it hasn't. There was some attempt at the midterm election. There was a pro forma committee in Congress, which has done nothing thus far. What are we? Three years later. This is shameful. The media, which is controlled by the great conglomerates which control the political system, has done an atrocious job of reporting. Though sometimes good stories get in. I've worn my eyes out studying the *Wall Street Journal*, which, despite its dreadful editorial policies, is a pretty good newspaper of record, which the *New York Times* is not. If you read the *Wall Street Journal* very carefully, you can pretty much figure out what happened that day. At the time of the first hijacking, according to FAA [Federal Aviation Administration] law, it is mandatory, within four minutes of hijacking, [that] fighter planes from the nearest military airbase go up to scramble; that means go up and force the plane down, find out who they are, find out what's happening. For one hour and fifteen minutes, I think it was, no fighter plane went up. During that hour and twenty minutes, we lost the two towers and one side of the Pentagon. Why didn't they go up? No description from the government, no excuse. A lot of mumbling stories, which were then retracted, and new stories replaced them. That, to me, was the end of the republic. We no longer had a Congress, which would ask questions, which it was in place to do, of the Executive. We have a commander-in-chief who likes strutting around in military uniform, which no previous commander-in-chief ever did, as they're supposed to be civilians keeping charge of the military. This thing is surrealistic now, and it is getting nastier and nastier. This government is culpable, if nothing less, of negligence. Why were we not protected, with all the airbases [and] fighter planes up and down the Eastern Seaboard? Not one of them went aloft while the hijackings took place. Finally, two from Otis Field in Massachusetts arrived at the Twin Towers. I think at the time the second one was hit. If anybody had been thinking, they would've gone on to Washington to try and prevent the attack on the Pentagon. They went back to Otis, back to Massachusetts. So, I ask these questions, which Congress should ask, does not ask; which the press should ask. But it's too frightened.

Also, in perpetual war for perpetual peace; there's another question that goes unanswered. The head of the Pakistan Secret Service was in Washington a week or so before 9/11. While he was there, and it was just a ceremonial visit with the head of the CIA, they work together . . . he sent back word to Islamabad for one of his henchmen to wire $100,000 to Mohammed Atta in the United States, which was duly done. The FBI—I think it was the *Wall Street Journal*, that's where I got this story from—only said American Secret Services found out about this. They complained to the Pakistani government. What is the head of your Secret Service in Washington telling to send $100,000 to a guy that we now know was the lead hijacker just a week before 9/11? *Times of India* published the whole story. The *Wall Street Journal* did a pretty good version for them. Now, shouldn't that be examined? Wouldn't Congress be interested in what this guy in Washington, meeting with all of our top secret people, says? "Okay, send him $100,000"? Not one more word. Not one more word. Now, in a country with any curiosity, in a public that was informed of anything, there would be a great deal of outcry. I couldn't imagine this happening in England. There'd be questions in Parliament. Papers would be full of it until it was solved. This couldn't happen in Italy, which dearly loves a conspiracy, or Germany. In the United States everybody listens to 19th-CENTURY FOX TV News, in which a bunch of loons just scream and scream and scream. And with each scream they tell another lie. How are we ever going to have an informed citizenry? Which means, then, how can we have an informed election?

UNTIMELY REFLECTIONS

ARNO MAYER: Well, I have the very bad habit of writing things for myself when there are some . . . when there is a major event and, more often than not, don't even think of submitting it to a journal or a newspaper—all the more so because if you write from a critical perspective—a fundamentally, radically critical perspective—it is relatively difficult, if not impossible, to get it into what is called the "media." So I wrote these critical reflections on September 11th, which in my judgment suggests that above all, the attacks on the Twin Towers and also on the Pentagon do bring down the curtain on the innocent American exceptionalism. And that really was my point of departure as someone born in Europe, as a refugee from Europe; of course, I had a different sort of relationship to the way in which one reflects about violence. I mean, this was a very violent act, and it's, at the same time, an infamous violent act. But at the same time, all things considered, if one keeps in mind the horrors of the 20th century—3,000 dead, though each of the victims needs to be remembered and needs to be memorialized—nevertheless, seen in a historical perspective, it struck me that 3,000 dead is not all that out of the ordinary . . . and I repeat, if one keeps in mind, you know, what the 20th century was all about. In any case, it also drove home, secondly, the fact that America during World War II, while so many other parts of the world and in particular Europe, experienced the elimination of what one could call the boundary between military personnel and civilians in wartime—the elimination of that boundary did not take place in the United States. For all intents and purposes, except the moment of Pearl Harbor, there were really no civilian casualties during World War II—American civilian casualties. And if you compare this to the experience of Europe, and you, needless to say, would also have to include Japan now, it is sort of mind-boggling that there should have been that exceptionalism at the very time when America nevertheless was very centrally involved in both World War I and World War II. The third thing that struck me as worth noting . . . is that some of the chickens are coming home to roost—that is to say that America has had an experience of sort of raising up Frankenstein leaders—in particular, in Third World countries—and then not quite knowing how, in one way or another, to clean up its act—the United States doesn't know how to clean up its acts. And in this particular case here, bin Laden, and from there you come to many other people who are being singled out for being the incarnation of evil—so many of them, we ourselves brought along.

In any case, once having written the article, [I] also insisted very strongly on the fact that there was one particularity to this moment. And that particularity is that there is really, in military terms, no counter-power to the American military. In other words, at the time that the notion of "superpower" was generally accepted, the idea was that there was more than one superpower—maybe there was, above all, . . . the Soviet Union. Since '89, that second superpower has disappeared and makes it all the more, in my judgment, . . . evident that America represents something other than a superpower, namely an empire. It is an informal empire that doesn't have a, shall we say, an imperial bureaucracy that has its representation, in . . . the outlying, shall we say, provinces of the American empire. It's an indirect rule, which is not to say that there are not the naval bases, the air bases, and so on and so forth. But still, it is an informal empire of the sort that, seems to me, does not really have a precedent in history. I'm inclined to say that even compared to the American empire, even the Roman Empire may be said to have been something in the nature of a tea party. In any case, having written the article, I tried to get it published, which is just another way to say that I sent it to a few journals, including to one journal that could be said to be on the left—no need to mention it by name—and it was not accepted there. It was not accepted in any number of places to which I sent it, and, out of the blue, I did send it to *Le Monde*, which decided to publish it. From there on, there were a few European publications that paid attention to it. But I hold no particular, I have no particular, how shall I say, stake in the article. . . . I wrote it . . . as I said, I wrote it first for myself and the only reason why it, how shall I say, was, I suppose, turned down by a number of places [was] because the expectation was that one would just uncritically rally around the flag. And it seems to me that it is the function of the critical intellectual to think analytically and the function of the historian to think contextually, even about those events that are the most unsettling and, at the same time, the most mobilizing around national symbols. And by virtue of that mobilization around national symbols, . . . all critical discussion [is simply eliminated].

APPENDIX

Since 1947 America has been the chief and pioneering perpetrator of "pre-emptive" state terror, exclusively in the Third World and therefore widely dissembled. Besides the unexceptional subversion and overthrow of governments in competition with the Soviet Union during the Cold War, Washington has resorted to political assassinations, surrogate death squads, and unseemly freedom fighters (e.g., bin Laden). It masterminded the killing of Lumumba and Allende; and it unsuccessfully tried to put to death Castro, Khadafi, Saddam Hussein (and bin Laden?). These "rogue" actions worsened local political and economic conditions and were of a piece with equally unscrupulous blockades, embargoes, military interventions, punitive air (missile) strikes, and kidnappings, always in the name of democracy, liberty, and justice. To be sure, for some of these actions America secured the sanction of the United Nations and the collaboration of NATO allies. At the same time, however, Washington refused to pay its dues to the United Nations, defied the nascent International Criminal Court, and condoned Israel's violation of international agreements and UN resolutions as well as its practice of preemptive state terror.

—Arno J. Mayer, Untimely Reflections, *September 2001*

Anti-war demonstration in Central Park, New York, October 6, 2002

". . . and the Pursuit of Happiness":
The Threat to Civil Liberties

Of all the enemies to public liberty, war is, perhaps, the most to be dreaded because it comprises and develops the germ of every other.
—James Madison, 4th US president (1809–1817)

NOAM CHOMSKY: It was immediately obvious, I think, my first interviews after 9/11, a few hours later, when journalists asked what I thought was going to happen, and I said what was obvious: that every repressive state in the world would use this as a window of opportunity to intensify acts of violence and repression. They would differ depending on the society. So, for Russia, it would mean stepping up the atrocious crimes in Chechnya, and for China, it would mean harsher repression in western China. For Indonesia, it would mean stepping up on Aceh. For Israel, it would be the occupied territories. . . . More repressive governments, like, say, Uzbekistan, would become even more totalitarian. The more democratic societies, like ours, would use the opportunity to impose greater discipline on our own populations and also to pursue their long-term objectives.

DONNA LIEBERMAN: Our government has launched a broadside against civil liberties. We see an administration that has attacked our criminal justice system by attacking the right to council. There are individuals held in detention without access to lawyers, without charges against them, with-

23

out even the prospect of a trial as a basis for determining guilt or innocence.

MICHAEL RATNER: After 9/11, the US government—the Bush administration, in particular—began a series of efforts, through law and administrative decisions, that substantially cut back on constitutional rights of people in the United States. They eventually passed a bill called the Patriot Act, which is misnamed. What it really is about is about taking away the rights of people in the United States.

CURT GOERING: The US Patriot Act I. There is really nothing patriotic about the US Patriot Act because it set in motion a restriction on liberties, which continue to be eroded until this day. And what that act did was allow the government to take some extraordinary steps, which have chipped away at our traditional civil liberties and human rights protection here in the United States.

MICHAEL RATNER: The Constitution, which protects our fundamental rights in the United States, is in great jeopardy. First, we have a clause of the Constitution called the 4th Amendment that protects the right to be free from government arrest without probable cause or without a reason. It protects the right of me not to be wiretapped without going to a court. It protects the right for me not to be stopped on the street and arrested. The 4th Amendment, I would say, has basically been crossed out of the United States Constitution.

REED BRODY: What the United States government seems to be doing in case after case is essentially anything it can get away with. If it can get away with trialing people in secret, it'll do that. If it can get away with not trialing people at all, it'll do that. If it can get away with putting people in a place like Guantanamo and then saying that they have no rights, that there is no court in the world to which these detainees can apply, then it will do that.

DONALD RUMSFELD (speaking at a Pentagon news conference in Washington, DC, January 24, 2002): The allegations that have been made by many from a comfortable distance, that the men and women in the US armed forces are somehow not properly treating the detainees under their charge, are just plain false.

> *US officials who take part in torture, authorize it, or even close their eyes to it can be prosecuted by courts anywhere in the world.*
> —Kenneth Roth, Human Rights Watch, December 2002

MICHAEL RATNER: Right now, we have six hundred and some people in Guantanamo Bay, Cuba. None of those people are being allowed into a court. None of them can challenge their jailing, none of them have access to an attorney, none of them have charges against them. That's not only happening in Guantanamo. We have American citizens now who are in jail here, a man named Hamdi and a man named Padilla, both of whom are American citizens and neither of whom are allowed to go into a court to challenge their convictions with an attorney that has ever met with them. They're both put in military brigs, not in regular jails, there's no charge against them, no contact with the families, nothing. Then we have a third large grouping of people that were picked up after 9/11, mostly immigrants from the Middle East. Estimates go from 1,200 to 3,000. They were put in jail, held incommunicado, without access to lawyers. We fought to get the names of those people who were arrested; government wouldn't give us the names. We fought to get access to them for attorneys; government wouldn't give us that. They're simply being held in jail. They've no relationship to terrorism. They're people who are your taxi driver, your flower seller, your doctor.

MONICA TARAZI: These individuals are not individuals who have been charged with any terrorist offenses. They are people who overstayed their visas, who have changed jobs without changing their visa status, this type of thing.

CURT GOERING: So, it was left to civil liberties groups and groups like Amnesty International who are contacted by families, sometimes by lawyers when detainees had access or were able to find a lawyer, although many of them did not. To try to piece together a picture of what was happening. It was a painstaking process. But we were eventually able to establish a pretty good sense of the treatment in detention—and in some places it was very bad, including isolation or solitary confinement for months at a time. Sometimes more than six or eight months, sometimes almost a year in solitary confinement.

MONICA TARAZI: There have been numerous cases of employment discrimination, for example, whereby an individual who has identified or been identified as Muslim or Arab-American has been terminated from their employment, or demoted, or had their hours reduced, or been harassed by fellow employees. We've seen quite a number of cases like that. We also recorded, as an organization, more than 700 violent incidents, targeting Arab-Americans, Muslim-Americans, South East Asians, and those perceived to be Arab and Muslim. And those types of incidents ranged from verbal abuse and name calling to more violent incidents, including actually a number of murders.

MICHAEL RATNER: Another part of the 4th Amendment right that has been taken away is the right to have your conversations not wiretapped by the government. Normally, . . . if the government wants to wiretap, let's say, my conversation, they have to go to the court and they have to say, 'We think Michael Ratner may have committed a crime and therefore we want a warrant to wiretap his phone line.' Instead, they go to the special Foreign Intelligence Surveillance Court that meets in a room that has all its windows blacked out, in the bottom of the Justice Department. No one is there except the judges on the court and someone from the US attorney's side or the United States government, and they issue warrants for people to be wiretapped. And they're issuing thousands of those warrants, thousands of them, and almost none are being issued by the regular procedures any longer under our Constitution. The second hallmark of the US Constitution, of our constitutional system and of any real democratic government, is the right to dissent and the right to tell your government what you think, the right to meet with other people in political groups and plan demonstrations, the right to write what you want. That's protected in the United States by the 1st Amendment to the United States' Constitution, which basically gives all of us, citizen and noncitizen alike, the right to petition our government and dissent, and they've basically made a huge inroad into that. And they've done it primarily through . . . releasing or unleashing, whatever word you want to use, the FBI and the CIA and other government intelligence agencies to spy in the United States on political and religious groups.

MONICA TARAZI: In the last couple of weeks, we've seen a new initiative coming out of the FBI, whereby district officers are being requested to count the number of mosques in their area. The implication being that Muslims are suspicious inherently because they're Muslim, and I think that that's a very dangerous message for the government to be sending.

JESSICA LANGE (speaking at the January 18, 2003, anti-war demonstration in Washington, DC): All this talk of war, all this rhetoric, has been an excellent cover, an excellent camouflage to turn back the clock on civil rights, on women's rights, on social justice, and in our environmental policies. And we have to ask, How far are they willing to go to silence the voice of dissent?

GORE VIDAL: The Patriot Act makes it possible for government agents to break into anyone's home when they are away, conduct a search, and keep the citizen indefinitely from finding out that a warrant was issued or not. They can oblige librarians to tell them what books anyone has withdrawn. If the librarian refuses, he or she can be criminally charged. They can also collect your credit reports and other sensitive information without judicial approval or the citizen's consent. Finally, all this unconstitutional activity need not have the slightest connection with terrorism. Early last month, the Justice Department leaked Patriot Act II, known as the Domestic Security Enhancement Act; as of January 9, 2003, it has not yet gone to Congress but it has certainly been leaked, when I saw parts of it. Here [are] some provisions: If an American citizen, a born American citizen, has been accused of supporting an organization labeled as terrorist by the government, he can be deprived of his citizenship even if he had no idea the organization had any link to terrorists. Provision in Act II is also made for more searches and wiretaps without warrant as well as section 201, secret arrests. In case a citizen tries to fight back in order to retain the citizenship he or she was born with, those federal agents who conduct illegal surveillance with the blessing of high administration officials are immune from legal action. A native-born American deprived of citizenship would, presumably, be deported—just as, today, a foreign-born person can be deported. Also, according to . . . American Citizens . . . this provision has some wonderful language. It says he is stripped of his citizenship, deported from the United States. Then they suddenly thought: "Well, what country would want him, you know. . . . We'd better rephrase this." Because of course he cannot get a passport as he doesn't have citizenship. So the thoughtful devisers of Domestic Security Enhancement authorize the attorney general to deport him "to any country or region regardless of whether the country or region has a government." Well it sounds like "Heaven" to me. . . .

> *In the end, we will remember not the words of our enemies, but the silence of our friends.*
> —Martin Luther King Jr.

LAURA VILD (reading the Not In Our Name pledge of resistance): We believe that as people living in the United States it is our responsibility to resist injustices done by our government in our name. Not in our name will you wage endless war. There can be no more deaths. No more transfusions of blood for oil. Not in our name will you invade countries, bomb civilians, kill more children, letting history take its course over the graves of the nameless. Not in our name will you erode the very freedoms you have claimed to fight for. Not by our hands will we supply weapons and funding for the annihilation of families on foreign soil. Not by our mouths will we let fear silence us. Not by our hearts will we allow whole peoples or countries to be deemed evil. Not by our will and not in our name. We pledge resistance. We pledge alliance with those who have come under attack for voicing opposition to the war or for their religion or ethnicity. We pledge to make common cause with the people of the world to bring about justice, freedom, and peace. Another world is possible and we pledge to make it real.

Molly Klopot: After 9/11, in March, a meeting was called of activists, peace workers, different people from various organizations to discuss what could be done in the present situation. And out of that grew both the NION pledge of resistance—the Not In Our Name pledge and the statement of conscience.

Not In Our Name Statement: Bush has declared: "You're either with us or against us." Here is our answer: NOT IN OUR NAME [Full-page entry in *New York Times* followed by a list of hundreds of names of people who endorsed it].

Molly Klopot: The statement of conscience was written by a number of intellectuals, actors, professors, and so on and has been endorsed. And the endorsement keeps growing and growing and has been published in a number of newspapers. The statement of conscience is going to be coming out again in the *New York Times* in a full two-page spread because it is getting so many endorsements.

Pete Seeger: One of the reasons I'm proud of America is we have a wonderful tradition of speaking your mind. It's in the Constitution. It says the Congress shall make no law . . . respecting the freedom of speech, freedom of religion, and so on. So whether you're right or wrong, you have a right. In fact, I used to sing it. *I may be right I may be wrong. Bring 'em home. Bring 'em home. I got a right to sing this song. Bring 'em home. Bring 'em home.* I sang that back during the Vietnam War.

Amy Goodman: There is a growing peace movement in this country and around the world. If only the media would cover it. Hundreds of thousands of people have marched, have gone out into the streets. And people don't just enjoy doing that. They'd rather go about their business and their lives. But they're doing it because no one has invited them into a studio to have a civilized discussion. They feel deeply about what is happening— that someone will be killed in their name, whether it is a US soldier or someone who is the target of a US soldier.

LESLIE CAGAN: Because the mainstream media doesn't really report on that, sometimes people feel they're isolated. They don't know, they don't know that they are really part of something bigger than themselves. And that can be very demoralizing. And that is one of the reasons why I think mass mobilizations are important. Not only for the message that they send to the powers that be. But [also because] it helps those people who come to a demonstration like that to feel connected, be connected to people. You see signs, you meet people from all over the country and different kinds of folks, different constituencies marching together. You begin to feel that you really are a part of something bigger than just yourself or just your small group. And that's very important—to get that sense of solidarity and connection.

PETE SEEGER: There has never been so many people trying to find some way to speak out for peace or sing out for peace, find something they can do. In small towns, not just big cities, but in small towns all around America there are peace vigils, women in black, you know, and some waving rainbow-colored signs. And the attempts by the government to diffuse it or mislead it have not really been successful. I'm personally positive, though I have no proof, that some of these people who do very angry things, throwing things, are literally, there is a French phrase, *agent provocateur*—somebody who wants to do a bad thing. And these people are sent in by the government to make the peace movement look silly. I have no proof of it, but I've known it's happened before. So, it's probably happening now.

MICHAEL RATNER: As the anti-war movement has grown by leaps and bounds, you're surely going to find the American government trying to suppress that movement. And what they'll do is they'll start to infiltrate the peace movement, they'll start to label the peace movement as tools of a foreign government, they'll start to accuse people of supporting Iraq or supporting terrorism, and they'll use a variety of ways to try and tarnish the peace movement, and one of those ways will be by the suppression of dissent, basically either criminalizing it or making it impossible, really, for people to get the word out, either through the media or otherwise.

PEOPLE ON THE STREET (addressing policemen as they were arresting anti-war demonstrators in Times Square, New York City, on March 20, 2003, the day the war started) : Peace! Now! What do we want? Peace! When do we want it? Now! Whose streets? Our streets! Whose streets? Our streets! Whose streets? Our streets! ...

KEN ESTEY: Every time there's repression abroad, there's repression here in the United States. The loss of freedoms for people abroad means the loss of freedoms for people here in the United States. If people care about freedom here, they've got to care about freedom somewhere else.

MOLLY KLOPOT: Because there is a link: If you're going to have a war on the world, you have to have a war on the people, you have to have a war on our civil liberties, you have to have a drive toward fascism. And we see that this is what has been happening.

> *There is a road to freedom. Its milestones are Obedience, Endeavor, Honesty, Order, Cleanliness, Sobriety, Truthfulness, Sacrifice, and love of the Fatherland.*
>
> —Adolf Hitler

EDMUND WHITE: I don't want to exaggerate, but I think there are comparisons between the United States now and the rise of Hitler in Germany. For instance, for the burning of the Reichstag, you have 9/11, which creates an emergency situation, which allows the government to justify abrogating lots of civil liberties and stifling opposition. Anybody who isn't for the government is declared unpatriotic. Then, just as Hitler had one war after another, in the same way, America is brewing these wars, especially the war in Iraq. So, that creates another crisis situation that requires lots of people in uniform to go someplace. And, again, you have to be patriotic and love the army and love our boys and you don't dare oppose any of that, or you're seen as a traitor. And then, just as Hitler stigmatized the Jews, in America I think we're stigmatizing Arab-Americans.

LESLIE KAUFFMAN (interviewed on February 7, 2003, in front of the US Federal Courthouse, downtown Manhattan, while a picket was taking place): Right now, there's a hearing taking place before Federal Judge Barbara Jones, where she's hearing our challenge to the city's refusal of a permit for the February 15th Anti-War March. There's a long, long history of big marches of many kinds in New York City and, on this occasion, the city is denying us a permit, which we believe is our constitutional right, to march on February 15th.

DONNA LIEBERMAN: The City of New York and the police department started to negotiate a route for a march and then abruptly they pulled the negotiations off the table. They pulled any proposals off the table and said, "No march, no place in New York City at any time on February 15th." The city has no problem with the St. Patrick's Day Parade, which draws 100,000 people or more, or the Israeli Day Parade, or the Puerto Rico Day Parade. It has no problem with them. But the city says that it's different when there is a political demonstration, that there are security concerns and time problems in getting the police together to handle a parade that is political and of this magnitude. What we saw was that tens of thousands of people never made it to the rally. [A] couple of hundred people were arrested for the crime of trying to get to the rally. People who were trying to make their way peacefully to the demonstration just never got there. And people poured out into the streets and at times it was wonderful, I'm told, and it was calm and peaceful. And at times the police charged with horses and people were hurt and people were arrested.

DONNA LIEBERMAN (speaking at the February 15, 2003, anti-war demonstration in New York City): They took away our right to march today. Well, looking out on this mass of humanity, all the way up 1st Avenue, all they way up 2nd Avenue, all the way up 3rd Avenue, the voices of dissent [have] not and will not be silenced.

LESLIE CAGAN (speaking at the February 15, 2003 anti-war demonstration in New York City): Shame on the City of New York! Shame on the Police Department! Shame on the Federal Courts! The people will be heard. We will not be silenced.

JULIAN BOND (speaking at the February 15, 2003, anti-war demonstration in New York City): Those of us gathered here today differ in many, many different ways, but by our presence here we share an enduring love of our country, an abiding faith in its institutions, its traditions, and its love of liberty. One of those traditions is the right, the responsibility, and the requirement to examine the actions of our leaders; to call them to account, to oppose them when they are wrong—and today they are wrong.

KATHA POLLITT: How effective is the peace movement? Well, sometimes I look at the political landscape and it seems to me the decision was made a long time ago to go to war in Iraq. Having very large protests is not going to affect the president's determination. . . . He said, . . . "Well, it's all very well that people demonstrate but I'm not making politics by focus group here." Now, the difference between a political demonstration and a focus group is quite considerable and, of course, he makes politics by focus group all the time.

MICHAEL FOLEY: I think if this movement is going to have any effect today on the Bush administration, it needs to think about how it can move as quickly as possible to methods and tactics, probably civil disobedience tactics, that are going to force this administration to change its policy.

CHESHIRE FRAGER: Civil disobedience for a person of faith is a question of leading; it is a witness; it is a testimony. So you don't just automatically do it. The individuals who are there on the other side are not your enemy, are not to be demeaned, are not to be insulted or provoked. No one else should be hurt, and probably no one else's property should be hurt.

SISTER ELIZABETH PROEFRIEDT: And for me that action is based in my faith and belief in the nonviolent Jesus. We need to speak to the legal system, which says that it's legal for our president to bomb women and children. That it's legal to have sanctions, that it's legal to have a preemptive war. And we sat yesterday. . . . I sat on the sidewalk of the UN for thirty seconds and prayed, and then I was arrested.

LESLIE CAGAN: It's more than a right; it's really an obligation to protest, and to make your objection public.

AMY GOODMAN: I think people will make an enormous difference if they speak out, and people should not be afraid to speak out. One should not be silent because they don't think their voice will have an effect. People do have an effect if they stand up, and just by standing up they are protecting those who are targeted right now.

RAMSEY CLARK (speaking at the House of the Lord Church in Brooklyn, New York, November 21, 2002): People have to stand up, they have to take to the streets, and they have to persevere until the government acts in accordance with the will of the people. That means no more militarism!

NOAM CHOMSKY: In the more free societies, we're lucky. It's not like Turkey, or Colombia, or Iraq, let's say. We're relatively free societies, we have a lot of privilege, lots of things we can do to affect government policy. If we have any commitment both to the issues and to democracy, [we] do it.

> *Did you, too, O friend, suppose democracy was only for elections, for politics, and for a party name?*
>
> —Walt Whitman

LIZA FEATHERSTONE: A lot of students have participated in broader community groups that have occupied the offices of congressional representatives when the Congress was about to vote on the Bush war resolution. You saw like here in New York, NYU [New York University] students occupied Hillary Clinton's office and you saw actions like that all over the country. There has really been a lot of protest on campus against the war in Iraq. We saw a brief wave of protest about the war in Afghanistan on campus, but the war on Iraq is really inspiring protest all over the country at more campuses that I have lost count [of]. . . . I counted over 400 but I know it's more. And it's many schools that have not traditionally been activists and haven't got involved in the anti-sweatshop movement or other movements that have been prominent. The issue is really galvanizing students. And many students who individually have not been active before. You see first-year students. You know, usually students take a little while to get used to college before they get active. This is really attracting kids who have just arrived at school. It's quite remarkable.

ANNA LANDAU (interviewed while organizing a trip with other Columbia University students to Washington, DC, to attend the anti-war demonstration on October 26, 2002): My name is Anna Landau. I am here with the Columbia anti-war coalition, and we are selling bus tickets to go to Washington, DC, for the national protest.

The following people were interviewed on the Columbia Anti-War Coalition buses heading to Washington, D.C., on October 26, 2002.

INTERVIEWER: So how can we make our voices heard?

GIRL: By doing things like demonstrations and protests.

BOY: A really big protest there, I think, is going to give a lot of people a sense like "I am not alone. . . ."

GIRL: We definitely need to protect our country from the horrible things that are going on right now, and the best way to do it is to be active.

GIRL: I do not agree with what the United States government is doing. I don't think it's right, I don't think it's acceptable, and I also think that it is my place as a citizen to speak out and say what I think is right.

LESLIE CAGAN: People should feel encouraged that so many people from so many different walks of life are speaking out.

The following people were interviewed in Washington, D.C., during the anti-war demonstration on October 26, 2002.

WOMAN: I am a member of the Community Church in New York.

BOY: I came here from Detroit.

MAN: Three-quarters of a mile off the street. I live on Capitol Hill.

MAN: From Pennsylvania—Northtown, Pennsylvania.

BUDDHIST MONK: From western Massachusetts.

MAN: I traveled from Brattleboro, Vermont.

BOY: New York City.

WOMAN: New York City.

OLD MAN: It looks like I have got plenty of company here. . . .

WOMAN: This president had this on his mind before he was elected. And now he's trying to push and bully all the American people into going to war. I'm strictly against it.

GIRL: Millions of people are against this war. So, definitely, we want to send the message out there.

MAN: I don't want war. I don't want the rest of the world just hating us because of his [Bush's] decision.

WOMAN: We in New York have been through a lot and, I tell you, we are not for war. The people of New York do not want war.

WOMAN: . . . To prevent life from being taken. It's very basic. The life I was given by God, and other people were given—nobody has a right to take that for any financial or [other] reason.

REV. JESSE JACKSON (speaking at the October 26, 2002, anti-war demonstration in Washington, DC): Say no to racism, but don't stop there. Say no to sexism, but don't stop there. Say no to anti-Semitism, anti Islamism. Say no to homophobia, but don't stop there. Our movement must reflect the healing and the values that we seek.

GEORGE W. BUSH (State of the Union speech, January 29, 2003): Whatever action is required, whenever action is necessary, I will defend the freedom and security of the American people.

REV. AL SHARPTON (speaking at the February 15, 2003, anti-war demonstration in New York City): You preach about homeland security. But this is our home and this is our land. This is the land of the people that get up and work every day, and we didn't work to send our children to foreign shores to protect oil interests. We work to have freedom and liberty and civil rights at home.

MICHAEL RATNER: And the government is saying, "We can make you safer if you give up your constitutional rights; if you let us surveille you, if you let us spy on you, if you let us wiretap you, if you let us throw immigrants in jail, we can make you safer." And as long as people feel threatened, they will let the government get away with this kind of cutbacks on our rights.

JOSE ALVAREZ: Prolonged arbitrary detention without any charge whatsoever on the basis that we don't know when this war will end is the very opposite of what the human rights movement is all about. And what I think this country has stood for for quite some time.

REED BRODY: Unfortunately the worst excesses here in the United States have come during times of war. During World War II the internment of Japanese-Americans in California, which is now looked on as a shameful part of our nation's history—we see it again since September 11th. The curtailment of human rights, probably the worst assault on the rights of noncitizens since World War II. Obviously, in times of national emergency, countries are going to step up security, and I think everyone agrees that the security of the population is paramount. But it can and should and must be done with the respect for liberties. To paraphrase Benjamin Franklin: Those who will sacrifice liberty for added security deserve neither liberty nor security.

JOSE ALVAREZ: Many of us who work in human rights consider that the age of rights that at least rhetorically we have supported, since World War II, after the Holocaust, is in grave danger. It's not just rights in the United States, it's human rights around the world. Part of the problem [is that, although] . . . we have been quite critical of civil rights and liberties being curtailed as a result of legislative actions like the US Patriot Act, we have not been as conscious in this country of the fact that what has been going on at the UN, that is, the terrorism sanctions imposed by the UN Security Council at the request of the United States, in and of itself, poses human rights problems around the world. What we are seeing is opportunism, by many states, that now say: "Look, terrorism made us do this." In fact we have seen human rights violators, once that we have identified for many, many years, now coming forward and saying: "We were right all along. Those security measures that we had adopted, those military courts that you had criticized, the rights of detention without trial that you had criticized—now, you see, we were right all along." And we are now seeing opportunists from China to Cuba, even, this is not a right-left question, coming forward and saying, "The Security Council made us do this" or "The US is leading the way in doing this."

REED BRODY: We see countries from Egypt to Uzbekistan to Russia and Chechnya to China using the anti-terrorism banner to repress their own people and to violate human rights.

GEORGE W. BUSH: The qualities of courage and compassion that we strive for in America also determine our conduct abroad. . . .

TV SCREEN (fake TV interruption): Sorry for the interruption. We are experiencing a temporary energy shortage due to another execution in Texas.*

CURT GOERING: Well, Amnesty International regards the death penalty to be a human rights violation because it violates the right to life. And particularly because it is carried out in some states in the United States against persons who are under 18 at the time the crime was committed. It's carried out against juveniles. It's carried out in many circumstances where there were serious questions about guilt or innocence. The death penalty in the United States is like a lottery system. It's more a function of race, of politics, of money than it is a function of the severity of the crime. Those who get the death penalty are almost invariably poor. They don't have a means to defend themselves or hire lawyers that are highly capable. And as a result [they] are stuck with court-appointed lawyers who sometimes fall asleep during the trial; who aren't in a position to prepare a vigorous and a quality defense. Those are the people who most often get the death penalty in the United States. But there is no way the system can be fixed. Worldwide, Amnesty calls for abolition of the death penalty. And there [are] great strides . . . being made in abolition worldwide. Over half the countries of the world now have abolished the death penalty in law or in practice. And over the past decade on average between two [and] three countries per year [have] abolished the death penalty. So, there is a definite worldwide trend. Right now it's about four countries that carry out 90 percent of the world's executions. China is by far the largest offender in this respect. And next are countries like Iran, Saudi Arabia, and the United States. Those are the countries that carry out about 90 percent of the executions in the world today.

> *One of the best ways to get yourself a reputation as a dangerous citizen these days is to go about repeating the very phrases which our founding fathers used in the great struggle for independence.*
>
> —Charles A. Beard

---

*While George W. Bush was governor of Texas, from 1995 to 2000, his execution chamber was by far the most active in the nation, killing 152 people—more than one prisoner every two weeks.

The qualities of courage and compassion that we strive for in America also determine our conduct abroad...

CLAP
CLAP
CLAP

Cartoon by Lorenzo Meccoli

GORE VIDAL: There is a quotation from Benjamin Franklin, and you cannot find it in any of the high school history books and not even in proper history books, except rarely. . . . Franklin has always been depicted as one of the great bores of the founding fathers, and he is of course one of the most interesting. In 1789 he was in Philadelphia for the making of the Constitution. He is old, dying. . . . And he finally read the work of his fellow conventioneers and he didn't like it. Then he thought about it and then he made a very interesting speech. He said: " I think that we should accept this Constitution for all of its errors and omissions"—at that time the Bill of Rights was not in there—"because it will give us for a course of years good government, which is what we need right now," and then "it may be a blessing to the people if well administered and I believe that this is likely to be well administered . . . and then only end due to the corruption of the people in despotism which will be the only form of government suitable for them." This is as dark a statement as anyone has ever made. They [history-book publishers] got around it. The best of the high school history books I saw—*American Pageant,* I think it was. It said that they were so afraid for Franklin. He kept going to dinner parties and his conversation was quite brilliant. They were terrified that he would give his true opinion on how this thing would end. So they had a couple of young men going around with him, sitting on either side. When Benjamin Franklin said, "Well, let me tell you about the Constitution . . ." they said, "Pass the salt to Mr. Franklin."

I thought of it, needless to say, when Franklin's prophecy came true in December 2000, when the Supreme Court bulldozed its way through the Constitution in order to select as their president the loser in the presidential election of that year. Despotism is now securely in the saddle. Is it due to the corruption of the people? Well, I thought: "What is corruption?" The founding fathers were always, many of them, on the verge of it; others in the Congress were. . . . The blankets didn't get to Valley Forge because it [the soldiers' request for more supplies during the winter of 1777–1778] couldn't pass Congress, it was sitting in Philadelphia. Corruption has always been with this, but why has it become so tall that you allow an election . . . and to make no contest? There was no outcry across the country when this terrible manipulation took place. And then of course Enron and Anderson; it was taken for granted that these great companies are like this. That CEOs are taking all the money that is not nailed down. And people out of work with no relief to fall back upon. So now I think what we might chat about is that despotism is really in the saddle. The old Republic is a shadow of itself, and we now stand in the glare of a nuclear world empire with a government that sees as its true enemy "we the people," deprived of our electoral franchise. War is the usual aim of despots, and serial warfare is what we are going to get unless—with help from well-wishers in new old Europe and from ourselves, awake at last—we can persuade this peculiar administration that they are acting on their own, and against all our history.

> *Men who have no respect for human life or for freedom or justice have taken over this beautiful country of ours. It will be up to the American people to take it back.*
>
> —Howard Zinn

HOWARD ZINN: There's always been a "they and we" in the United States. We pretend that that isn't so. In the United States, we pretend that there are no classes. We pretend that there's just one interest that covers us all. We pretend to a common interest. We use words, phrases, like "the national interest," "national security," "national defense," as if we all have the same national interests, we all have the same security. No, we always, in this country, from the very founding of this nation, even before the founding of this nation, always had differences of interest. There's always been a slave-owning class, a merchant class, an industrial class, and there's always been a wage-earner class, a slave class, a servant class—and American history is full of class conflict. Now, the textbooks in American history don't want to talk about that, but we've always had conflict, right from the beginning. I mean, the American Constitution was founded in order to control class conflict. The founding fathers, James Madison, and . . . they said this very explicitly. They want . . . They need to control the conflict that occurs between people who own property and people who don't own property. So, from the beginning, we've always had classes, we've always had class conflict. And so, there's always been a "they." The "they" consists of the political leaders of the country who are in close connection with the business interests of the country, the corporate interests, who are in close connection with the military. You will see the same people going back and forth from the government to the military to the corporations. People leave the government and they take jobs in big corporations. People are retired generals and they're immediately given jobs as CEOs of major companies that will then do business with the Pentagon. . . . So, there's a very close connection there . . . between these three groups—the political, the military, the corporate. And, that's the "they." Now the "we" is everybody else. The "we" is 95 percent of the American people, or maybe 99 percent of the American people. But the . . . people . . . don't benefit from this control of the wealth, and this control of the government by this small elite.

Making a peace sign with small stones, anti-war demonstration, Central Park, New York, October 6, 2002

".. . and Nothing But the Truth":
Journalism in Crisis

Half the American population no longer reads newspapers: plainly, they are the clever half.

—Gore Vidal

PETE SEEGER: Plato is supposed to have said [in *The Republic*] that it's very dangerous to allow the wrong kind of music. . . . And there's an old Arab proverb that says: "When the king puts the poet on his payroll, he cuts off the tongue of the poet." I think that every time I get a job on TV.

LESLIE CAGAN: The media has become an extremely powerful force in people's lives. And by force I mean, it is [not only] where people . . . get their news about what's going on in their community and in their world and everything in between, but also where people get a lot of the ideas about who they are and what their place in society is.

RACHEL COEN: Democracy basically cannot work without an informed citizenry. And in a country the size of the US that means you need an aggressive, independent news media. Citizens are going to make their political decisions and calculations based on information. And most of the ways that we get our information is through our mainstream media. When that information is bad, false, partial, distorted, then it is going to interfere with the workings of democracy. People aren't going to be informed, aren't going to be able to be full participatory citizens.

41

KATHA POLLITT: If all you read was the *New York Post*, if all you read was the *Daily News*, you would have no materials, no information with which to ... begin to get a different perspective. And not only that, most people don't read any newspaper, most people watch television!

DANNY SCHECHTER: There is more punditry on television. That is to say, [more] opinionizing than journalism. So, there [are] more argument shows, shout shows, people yelling at each other; less light, more heat. There's been a merger of news biz and show biz, so that entertainment values are infiltrating all the news coverage. As a consequence, there's less background, less context, less analysis, and more image-driven information, which often can be very misleading, inaccurate, and just plain wrong.

EMILY REINHARDT: People associate the news with *Entertainment Tonight* or *Access Hollywood* or whatever. I mean, they sit at anchor desks, so it looks kind of like the news. The news is dedicated a lot more to those kind of featuresque stories that are a lot more celebrity reporting. Monica Lewinsky, Gary Condit, O. J. Simpson to a certain extent, Robert Blake. There's just tons of them. And in the case of someone like Monica Lewinsky, Americans have to look and say; Well, Osama bin Laden was out there at that time, you know. There [were] a lot of things happening in the world and there always are a lot of things happening around the world that we were caught up in, whether our president was getting a blowjob or not.

EDMUND WHITE: There is this thing called the "dumbing down of America," in which fewer and fewer people read books, fewer and fewer people are interested in intellectual issues. So, I think that that probably reduces the power of intellectuals even more. But, there are very few Americans who would even describe themselves as intellectuals, even those who are professors, or writers, or painters, or whatever—they would never say, "I'm an intellectual." It's considered embarrassing to say that in America.

GORE VIDAL: The idea of geography is very exciting to people because I think it's only 7 percent of the American people [who] have passports. Only 7 percent have been abroad, not counting the ones who are sent in the military, of course. But 7 percent have voluntarily gone abroad. It's a tiny percent of those in Congress who have been abroad. Bush had never set foot in Europe before he became president. He spent 10 minutes in China when his father was ambassador there and obviously never went outside the compound. What I have to do a lot of times in Europe is explain to them, "No, Americans are not stupid." They think, when they meet them, they think they're very stupid because they don't know anything. I said, "They're not stupid at all"; as a matter of fact, I think we're rather brighter than the average, but we're ignorant, which means not knowing. We have no information because it isn't given to us. Our public schools are a scandal. They stopped teaching geography in 1950 in most of the public schools, by which time we were a global empire. We have a global empire and nobody knows where anything is. Nobody knows any languages. So, our statesmen go abroad and people laugh at them because they are so dumb or seem to be so dumb.

> *The best way to get the news is from objective sources. And the most objective sources I have are people on my staff.*
>
> —George W. Bush, 43rd US president

SUSAN SARANDON (accompanied by Tim Robbins, speaking at the October 6, 2002, anti-war demonstration in New York City): I am so very happy to be here. I have been feeling so isolated, so lonely, so convinced by the mainstream media that I'm out of my mind to be worried about this path that we are taking towards this war. Look around you and see how many people are here today, because I guarantee you it will not be represented this way when you read about it in the morning.

AMY GOODMAN: There is a growing movement in this country that is not only protesting war, [it is] protesting the media that beats the drums for war.

YOUNG MAN IN ONE OF THE COLUMBIA ANTI-WAR COALITION BUSES (heading to the October 26, 2002, anti-war demonstration in Washington, DC): Most people have to rely on mainstream newspapers and news and [these are] terrible, especially about foreign policy stuff. Black is white and up is down. It's the opposite of the truth. So I think most people, despite having very little access, are already suspicious of this war and, if they actually had more access, would totally be against it.

ANOTHER YOUNG MAN IN ONE OF THE COLUMBIA ANTI-WAR COALITION BUSES: You have people like Cheney or Rumsfeld saying outrageous things every day and you want journalists to ask one difficult question. How about a half-difficult question? Nothing. It's complete carte blanche for the government. They are not even talking to anybody who opposes the war, people in the anti-war movement. It's a very one-sided picture. So it doesn't really help a lot of ordinary people who are confused, not really sure why we are attacking a country that hasn't attacked us. The media doesn't help.

US Secretary of Defense Donald Rumsfeld

The following people were interviewed during the October 26, 2002, anti-war demonstration in Washington, D.C.

INTERVIEWER: How much faith do you place in the media?

YOUNG MAN: In the media? None.

INTERVIEWER: How much faith do you place in the administration?

WOMAN: None!

INTERVIEWER: And in the media?

WOMAN: None!

MAN: The US media has just become a propaganda machine. That's a fact. There's nothing objective about it whatsoever at this point. So watching CNN or reading the paper is like listening to the White House administration from another point of view.

INTERVIEWER: How do you think the media is going to portray this event?

ANNA LANDAU: I definitely don't think they're going to portray it as big as it is. There's a *lot* of people here and they're not going to show that. They might say there was a protest. They got to say there was a protest, but they're not going to say it's as big as it is.

RACHEL COEN: October 26th, there was a major anti-war march in Washington, DC. Outlets like the *Washington Post* and the *LA Times* ran big headlines and estimated the crowd size around 100,000 people, also noting that this far exceeded the organizers' expectations. You know, they got a really big turnout. The *New York Times*, however, and the National Public Radio ran rather different stories. According to them there were a few thousand people there and organizers were disappointed with the small turnout.[1]

TONY MURPHY: We had a huge crunch backstage of TV cameras, newspaper reporters. I was the media coordinator. I was answering phone calls every five minutes in the days leading up to October 26th. There were several reports from some major news outlets like *New York Times* and National Public Radio, which, in their initial reports, reported a few thousand people. We called the *New York Times* and we said: "Why did you print this article?" and they really weren't interested in talking to us.

RACHEL COEN: We issued an action alert to our e-mail list, which went out to about 32,000 or 33,000 people. And within a day, there were hundreds and hundreds of letters being written to the *New York Times* and NPR asking them to please correct this coverage. Interestingly enough, the *New York Times* never ran a formal correction. But three days later, on October 30th, they ran a second follow-up article. The editor and publisher described it as a "makeup" piece, noting the correct size of the rally, noting that the organizers were pleased with the turnout, and it just stood in direct contradiction to their earlier piece. NPR, for its part, both updated the piece on the air and issued a formal apology on the website, formally correcting the error.[2]

LESLIE CAGAN: And I think people come to understand that part of our work has to be keeping the pressure on the media as well as on the government in order to get the story out there.

AMY GOODMAN: We understand in this country that it takes media activism. That the media [are] a part of the establishment and they have to be ripped from it, to follow what should be their original mission, and that is to report the truths, many truths of people who believe, have many different views of what should happen right now.

RACHEL COEN: I think that undercounting crowd sizes at popular demonstrations and particularly at peace demonstrations is a very common error, enough so that it is a trend in the mainstream media.

JULIA WILLEBRAND: Those of us who are activists just have to see how the *New York Times*, which is *the* national newspaper, covered two anti-war demonstrations—the one on October 26th and the one two weeks ago on January 18th. They knew perfectly well that there were [at least] a hundred thousand people . . . there on October 26th, and yet they said several thousands in their coverage. Two weeks ago, on January 18th, the *New York Times* reported tens of thousands. The police chief of Washington, DC, estimated 200,000. So, they're just symptoms of a media that is now controlled by multinational corporations doing the bidding of the corporations that own them.

LESLIE CAGAN: In the early days of the anti-war movement the media actually covered it a fair amount and that's how we knew that things were happening. They covered when students would walk out of classes, out of college; now they hardly cover that. There is a lot of campus stuff going on and the mainstream media hardly covers it. So one of the ways that the movement grew was because the mainstream media was covering it. At a certain point I think that they [the media] realized that they were servicing us and helping us. And the coverage stopped or changed. And certainly in the last several years of the anti-war movement, there was often . . .

what they would show was like the most fringe people. People who wore kind of the most outrageous outfits, who weren't dressed like mainstream Americans. Or people who had the weirdest signs or the most inflammatory signs. That's what the picture would be, or something like that. And also one thing is that while the media would often cover some of the stuff that the anti-war movement was doing, they wouldn't always get it right about what the content was and about what the message was. Often it was portrayed as kind of anti-America. Where really it wasn't so much anti-America as it was anti-US policy and "anti–this war" that the United States was carrying out.

MICHAEL FOLEY: I think the media's coverage of today's movement is very similar to the way it covered the anti-war movement during the Vietnam War. For the most part, the media, when it covered draft resisters or any kind of large demonstrations during the Vietnam War, focused on the most outrageous looking and the most outrageous behaving activists they could find. The mainstream, middle-aged, or older protesters who came out with their children, for example, never appeared in photographs or in stories in the mainstream press. That seems to be happening today as well.

MICHAEL RATNER: One thing that happened recently, I along with 100 other law professors, sent a letter to President Bush, and so did lawyers in the UK send one to Blair, and the lawyers in Canada sent one to Prime Minister Chretien, about if they fight a war with Iraq, having to obey the Geneva Conventions, and not bomb civilians and bomb the electrical grid, and they put us on TV on one of the cable channels and the lead was "Can you believe this?" You know, "Look what these nutty lawyers are doing." And then they have the debate with the person who disagrees with us. It's fine that they had the debate with someone who disagreed with us, but they characterized the whole program as if we were nuts. This is after the Bush administration, the first Bush administration, essentially violated the Geneva Conventions all over the place with regard to what it did to Iraq in '91, and then we send the letter and they say *we're* crazy.

DANNY SCHECHTER: One of the anti-war groups, Not In Our Name, produced an ad and they offered it to MTV. MTV rejected the ad. They did cover it in MTV News, but they wouldn't broadcast it. Even though the group offered them money, and even though MTV originally agreed to broadcast it. So, the group was able to bypass MTV by buying time on the cable systems, which carry MTV and distribute MTV. So, it has gotten out in some cities and in some markets. But it's an uphill battle. Why should people with anti-war points of view have to buy time, buy ads in newspapers, buy time on TV to get their voices heard? Why aren't they being heard as part of the national debate? That's the question.

AMY GOODMAN: There have been more than a million people who have marched in Italy. In Britain in one protest alone, there were 400,000 people. And they were addressed by the likes of John Pilger, the well-known Australian filmmaker who lives in Britain; the mayor of London, Ken Livingstone; the parliamentarian, George Galloway, who has been to Iraq a number of times. They were addressed by Scott Ritter, the former UN weapons inspector, and many others. That protest is very significant. It didn't get covered by the *New York Times* or the *Washington Post*. They did cover a protest the week before, that occurred in Britain that had the same number of people. It was for fox hunting.

MONICA TARAZI: The media has been quite irresponsible, I think, in the portrayal of the Arab and Muslim community. There have been numerous examples of television shows and news programs which have been extremely irresponsible and this has included having so-called "experts" on the Arab world or Islam, making some quite appalling statements, which are able to go unchallenged. It's included, for example, talking about terrorism and using the imagery of Muslims at prayer, which is quite an insidious . . . sends a very bad message that praying is inherently linked to terrorism, which is, obviously, very problematic.

RACHEL COEN: It is a film based on a memoir. So it is not a documentary, but it has been advertised as the real story, the true behind-the-scenes story. That is sort of how HBO is promoting it. It is called "Live from Baghdad." And it is about the CNN coverage of the 1991 Gulf War. The scene in question, that FAIR issued an action alert about, was about a story widely circulated both by the media and by the US government during the first Gulf War about Iraqi soldiers coming into a Kuwait hospital and pulling infants out of incubators, sort of leaving them on the ground. Implication being either that they were killed or severely injured, or something like that. A Kuwait girl testified before Congress about having witnessed this as an atrocity. And it was one of the major motivators of getting people behind the war effort, this terrible thing Iraqi troops did. The movie "Live from Baghdad" retells this story and sort of shows the CNN news team going in and trying to get the real scoop on it, finding out what happened. It is sort of unresolved in the movie, but most viewers, I think, would be left with the impression that this had occurred and that the Iraqi government was trying to use CNN for its own propaganda, to deny it. In fact, the story was a PR concoction, but it was a PR concoction probably of the

Kuwaiti government [and] perhaps the US. There is a well-known PR firm called Hill & Knowlton that was behind it, and after the war was over it was debunked. We now know that it didn't happen. So when HBO announced this film airing, which had portrayed this as the truth, we issued a media advisory and action alert about it. It is difficult to speculate on the motivations of HBO. We did have questions about the motivation for the movie in general. It almost functions as a commercial for CNN. And CNN and HBO are owned by the same corporate parent, AOL Time Warner, which raised some ethics concerns for us.

GREG PALAST: I have been investigating what has been going on in Venezuela. I've not only met with the president . . . of Venezuela, Hugo Chavez. But I met with the people who kidnapped him back in April. I met with both sides. I've been in the streets. I've been trying to find out what's going on. I've met with OPEC members, trying to find out what's going on. [The] *New York Times* runs a picture on the front page of thousands of people demonstrating in the streets against Hugo Chavez. And I was in Caracas. I saw those people demonstrating. No question they were there, OK. What they didn't show is that across town, there was a demonstration, which was bigger for Hugo Chavez. In other words, they literally sliced the picture so that you got a false story. And in that case, you know, you had a picture that was worth a thousand lies because people see a picture and they believe, "Well, you can't fake a picture. It's the truth." But the picture was true. Thousands of people marching against the president of Venezuela, but they didn't say more people are marching *for* him. So, the picture was, in effect, fabricated propaganda—complete, absolute nonsense. And they put out the story, for example, that Hugo Chavez resigned as president. Where did they get that? . . . I could ask them about that too. They said, "Oh, we got it from the US State Department." As if that's an acceptable source. And they ran it as true. They didn't even say, "The US State Department asserts . . . " or "We got this from the US State Department." No identification of the source. Simply reprinting official state propaganda, which was nothing but a bunch of garbage, crap, nonsense, baloney, [a] fabricated lie end to end. And a dangerous lie because by saying that Hugo Chavez, who is being held hostage, had resigned, it gave legitimacy to a coup d'état. Now, if Chavez had been killed we'd have never known the truth.[3]

ARNO MAYER: After there had been a particularly violent sort of incident in the Israeli-Palestinian conflict . . . and I'd written a piece on settlements and sort of making what, to me, was the self-evident point, namely, that there was no way of coming to an accommodation in between Israel and the Palestinians without the elimination, the collapse, of the settlements. So I didn't think I was writing anything particularly radical or militant, but nevertheless, that piece was turned down everywhere, even to the point where a major European publication, a weekly—I won't give the name—sort of wrote back to say that they couldn't publish it and gave a number of reasons and so on and then the editor added a P.S. at the bottom of the letter—because I happen to know him personally—and [he]then said: "Of course you realize that I totally agree with your position, but I fear that I can't publish it."

LARRY HOLMES (speaking at the House of the Lord Church in Brooklyn, New York, November 21, 2002): You know, thirty-five years ago, Martin Luther King said in his famous speech where he came out against the war, a quote that I know many of you know: "The United States is the greatest purveyor of violence in the world today." Now, that was 1967. But yet, if Martin Luther King were alive today and went on FOX and said that, they'd ridicule him. They'd arrest him. . . . They'd say: "You're out of the mainstream. We gave you a Nobel Peace Prize, we fought and won a birthday for him." But you can just imagine what all the talking heads would call him: "Well, you can't say that. It's unpatriotic. Shut him up!"

DANNY SCHECHTER: Ever since 9/11, September 11th, the American media has tended to try to be patriotically correct, not to get ahead of the viewers. They've tried to pander to the viewers . . . and they've often served as an echo chamber, a megaphone for the government and government positions. And they've tended to cover the news in a very pro-administration way [that] was excluding critics, excluding other points of view. This is dangerous for a democracy because people are not being given all sides. They're not being . . . given the information they need to make up their own minds about what's happening. There's been a lot of manipulation. There's been a lot of censorship. And there's been a lot of self-censorship.

RACHEL COEN: After the September 11th attacks, newscasts . . . became wrapped in the flag, both broadcast and cable TV news. They developed different flag graphics to literally frame their newscasts in. Many anchors or reporters started wearing flag lapel pins. It was really overwhelming and, in our book, inappropriate. We had figures like Dan Rather, one of the best-known, most-respected newspeople in the country; he went on the Letterman Show, a late-night talk show, and said basically, "Mr. President, just tell me where to line up." And he started crying. It was this very emotive, extensible patriotic display.

KATHA POLLITT: There was no distinction made after 9/11 between trying to understand a political phenomenon and thinking it was a good thing, you know. And people who tried to do that, people who said, "Let's think about why this is happening," were called unpatriotic. Susan Sontag, for example, wrote, you know, a 500-word piece—a little edit for the *New Yorker*—in which she said, "Look, they're not cowards," and also, "We should think about why . . . why this is happening, what this represents" . . . and, "Oh my God, she's so anti-American, she's so hostile to all our values, she's terrible, she's apologizing for them." You could not try to understand something without seeming to apologize for it, and I think it took months and months and months before it was possible to ask the questions that the rest of the world was asking right away.[4]

GEORGE W. BUSH (State of the Union speech, January 29, 2003): In a whirlwind of change and hope and peril, our faith is sure, our resolve is firm, and our union is strong.

MICHAEL RATNER: I watched the State of the Union speech that took place and it was the most fawning, adulatory media response that I've ever seen. They all talked about Bush being determined and square-jawed and giving a great speech and really being unwavering and made him into this . . . Caesar addressing the Roman Senate, which is what it was like. It was like Caesar talking about empire to the Roman Senate. . . . I didn't see one commentator who was critical at all of that scene. Of course you had all of our congresspeople and senators clapping away, etc., etc.

DANNY SCHECHTER: President Bush gave a press conference. It was his 8th press conference since he's been in office. By this time Bill Clinton had given thirty press conferences, the same amount of time in office. So, he doesn't give many press conferences. And this press conference seemed to be very managed. The president had a certain message. He repeated it no matter what question he was asked. He spoke very slowly. He talked a lot about his faith, his personal convictions, why Saddam Hussein was a bad guy. But he often didn't even answer a lot of the questions. But worse, I think, than all of that, the press corps didn't ask him very strong questions. There was a tendency to try to be nice, to ask him you know what we call "softball" questions; not really tough questions. And as a result, I think the whole situation was a charade of journalism. It was a disgrace.

GREG PALAST: Dan Rather was on my program. There was another reporter talking to him—[from] *News Night* in BBC Television in London. And he told the British audience, "We can't ask questions in America. We know we should be asking tough questions. I know I ought to be asking tough questions. But I don't because I'd be lynched. I'd be killed." That's what he said. "If I ask questions, people call me unpatriotic. That's what they'd call me." So, Dan Rather, one of the most powerful American television journalists, can't tell the truth. He's afraid of asking a question. Can you imagine?[5]

DANNY SCHECHTER: His interview was the number-one story in almost every British newspaper the next day. It wasn't even covered by any American papers. It was a small little celebrity quote in the *Los Angeles Times*. That was all I could find. We also had a situation where one of our top investigative reporters, Seymour Hersh, well known for investigating the My Lai massacre in Vietnam and . . . Watergate . . . many big stories. He was attacked as a terrorist by Richard Perle, one of the president's top advisors; [he] called him a terrorist because [Hersh] was criticizing the fact that Richard Perle is investing in companies that are involved in homeland security while he's an advisor to the president, saying it's a conflict of interest. So he gets branded as a terrorist.[6]

They came up with a new idea of co-opting journalists, what they call "embedding" them, putting them into the military units, where they would get to know the soldiers. The story would shift from a policy story to a human-interest story—profiling the soldiers, where they're from and the rest of it. Now, many other people feel this is dangerous, that it's like not embedding but "getting in bed with" the military. This is something that threatens independent coverage of the war.

HOWARD ZINN: Putting the reporters into the army . . . giving them uniforms, giving them training, and having them go along with the soldiers? I mean, this is a very clever device to bring the reporters close to the military. And, you know, they'll be friends with the military. They'll be friends with the generals and the colonels, and they will be watched closely about what they report about the war. So, no, the media in the United States is not an independent media.

CURT GOERING: And that's why we can see the Bush administration propagating lies, in effect—maintaining that there [has] been documented evidence of weapons of mass destruction and yet not able to produce them after it's been in the country for more than a month now. It's why they're able to make the case that there is a link between the Iraqi government and

Anti-war demonstration in Central Park, New York, October 6, 2002

Al-Qaeda. And the public believes there is a link even though there is no evidence. No evidence has been produced of that link.

HOWARD ZINN: And one of the reasons [Bush is] able to do this is because the media—the major media, television, major newspapers, radio stations—they have cooperated with the Bush administration. They have not been bringing out the 2000 election. They have helped create an amnesia about the 2000 election. They have not gone into the history of American policy in the Middle East. They have not been talking about oil. They do not go back to the, you know, coup in Iran in 1953; they don't give any of that history. So, with the cooperation of the media, the Bush administration has succeeded in diverting the attention of the American public from the election of 2000, from the failure of the bombing of Afghanistan, from the question of oil.

CURT GOERING: News networks like FOX television in effect act as a mouthpiece for the government, [so] that you can't really distinguish between a government press conference with government spokespeople and FOX anchors sometimes. And this is a network that more and more is gaining [an] audience in the United States. So, it's a very discouraging situation here, where more and more people are receiving their news in this kind of fashion and are as a result less and less informed. And the government is able to get away with an agenda, which is not grounded often in fact or in truth. And with the power that it has, you know, that's a dangerous combination.

> *One of the things we don't want to do is to destroy the infrastructure of Iraq . . . because in a few days we are going to own that country.*
> —Tom Brokaw, NBC, March 20, 2003

NORMAN SOLOMON: The journalist Ben Bagdikian, a former assistant managing editor of the *Washington Post,* did a book that was first published in 1983 called *The Media Monopoly.* At that time he documented that fifty corporations, through ownership, control most of the news and information flow in the United States. Fast-forward two decades: by the year 2000, that number had dropped to six, you know, and [is] still dropping. Well, that involves concentration of media ownership with de facto political and economic power. It reflects that power and it reinforces it. [See Appendix.]

LESLIE CAGAN: A few corporations really control the media and control the news outlets right now in this country. And there has been just a narrowing of space in the media, and that's why the fight to hold on to Pacifica was so important, because there are so few outlets, be they print or electronic outlets, where you hear alternative voices—where you hear, not just challenges to the policies and the status quo, but places where you can hear other ideas of how life could be different.

AMY GOODMAN: The mainstream media beats the drums for war, the mainstream media profits from war. The corporations that own the media, let's look at the Persian Gulf War. In 1991, Westinghouse owned CBS, General Electric owned NBC. These were two of the major weapons manufacturers. They made most of the parts for most of the weapons during the Persian Gulf War.

HOWARD ZINN: Well, you know the American media is not a very democratic institution. The media are concentrated in a few hands. The few powerful media giants control most of the major television stations, most of the major newspapers. Most cities in the United States have only one newspaper—no competition really. And these media giants have very close connections with the government in Washington, and they have a tremendous lobbying effort. They are the ones who succeeded in getting the Telecommunications Act of 1994 passed by Congress, signed by President

Clinton. The Communications Act enables the major media to acquire even more and more of the media outlets in the United States. So, you know, this is a . . . billionaire-owned media, and their interests are close to the interests of corporate America and close to the interests of the American government. So, they have been doing what the American government wants.

KATHA POLLITT: I think this country has moved . . . the center has moved very far to the right. And my theory is always that the president determines where the center is and so the more conservative the president is, everybody kind of just moves over—"I guess it should be this way." Everybody just moves over a little bit more to the right. And so we moved a little bit back with Clinton and now it's moving way to the right—just way over there. "Is there still a left in the United States?" Well, you know, if you had asked me this question a year ago, I would have said, "Essentially, no." That what there *is* is . . . a collection of loosely friendly single-issue groups. There's the environment, there's feminism, there's racial justice. A few years ago, not so much now, there was a lot of activity in solidarity with Latin American liberation movements. But a year ago, it did seem to me that there wasn't anything really that you could call a left that was more than 3,000 people in the whole country—I picked that number out of a hat. But today, I think that it's a little different—that a number of things together have really wakened people up and one of them is the prospect of this war and the other is the Bush administration. You'll remember that when the election was in dispute, a lot of people thought, "Well, . . . if [Bush] becomes the president, . . . he was elected by the minority of the people and he'll be aware of that, he'll govern from the center, he'll be moderate, he'll have to placate all those angry Democrats out there." Not a bit of it! He took the ball, and like the Republicans always do, they take the ball and they run with it as far as they can. It's only the Democrats who say, "Oh my goodness, a lot of people don't like me, I better not do anything. I better try to make those people who don't like me happy." No, the Republicans, they say, "We've got four years at least, you know, and we're going to go after abortion, we're going to go . . . you know . . . we're going to do all kinds of things for conservative Christians, we're going to take this homeland security thing as far as we can, we're going to invade people's civil . . . you know, do what we want with people's civil liberties, we're going to do what we want with so-called Tort Reform and all kinds of pro-business legal things, we're going to change . . . cut the taxes of rich people and we're just going to do that." And, I think that that's beginning to sink in. . . . Now that the Republicans control the White House, Congress,

[and] still the majority of governorships and many state legislatures, with the Supreme Court in play, I think that people are beginning to say, "Wait a minute here, these people are way too conservative for us, this isn't what we wanted." And, I think even some people who voted for Bush may come to feel that way.

EDMUND WHITE: It's a difficult period, and what surprises me is that there isn't more opposition. I think it's partly that . . . through probably an accident, an unhappy accident, there are no significant leaders on the left. So, we just don't happen to have any good, powerful, magnetic people. It's partly because politics is so corrupt in America, and so much an affair of money and big business, that I think that a lot of talented and intelligent and dynamic people don't go into politics anymore. It's not a good field to be in, especially if you're on the left. It's just hard to get the financing to run. So, anyway, it seems to me very much that . . . that there are lots of different leftist causes that are being violated by the present government. I mean there's a whole array of things. The environment is being destroyed by the Bush administration. The black affirmative action has been revoked. Big business is being favored through the new tax plan, and the rich are being favored at the expense of the poor. The anti-war movement is very strong. The gays . . . certainly have no friends in Washington right now. So, it seems to me that in every area that you could say composes the left traditionally, there are people who are watching their rights being eroded. And I think that it would be natural to expect all of these groups to come together and form a new coalition against the Bush administration, but there's very little press on the left.

AMY GOODMAN: So especially in a time of war it is important to bring out independent voices, voices of dissent. And I think that those voices don't represent the marginalized fringe; they don't represent even the silent majority, but the silenced majority. Silenced by the mainstream media.

NOAM CHOMSKY: They're not independent systems. They're part of a system of domination and power. That's true institutionally, that's true ideologically, that's true of [the] cultural background of the people who participate, and they, by and large, serve that purpose. So, they're doing their job. . . . Well, let's take some concrete case: Take this famous "new Europe/old Europe" business. Okay, so the old Europe, which we denounce, is France and Germany; and new Europe, which is with us, is Italy and Spain and Hungary and so on. Well, you know, to do their job properly, the media have to point out, have to not fail to point out, that in Italy and Spain and Hungary, opposition to the war is even higher than it is in France and Germany. They have to suppress that. You know, it's true—I mean, the countries know it's true. And . . . what they also have to fail to say is that . . . we despise democracy. We hate it with such a passion that we will call a leader—Berlusconi, say—we'll say, "He's on our [side]. . . . His country is on our side, if he hates democracy as much as we do, and therefore he follows our orders, over the objection of 85 percent of his population." In that case, he's a good guy. That expresses contempt for democracy in such a brazen form that it's, you know, hard to think of any counterpart. And that has to be suppressed . . . and it is. I mean, occasionally you'll see a hint saying, "Well, some Europeans don't like us" or something. But they don't present it . . . and, in fact, the extent of suppression is impressive.

And, so, take for example, the Gallup polls—not an obscure organization exactly. Gallup International did a poll on Europe . . . in January—you know what result it showed. I mean, it showed that, for the war that both Bush and Blair are announcing—namely, "We'll go in ourselves with a coalition of the willing"—the highest support in all of Europe was 11 percent in Romania, mostly lower than that . . . for most of the countries. It's 75 percent [in] Spain-"We don't want to go to war even though the UN authorizes it." But for support of the war they're talking about . . . [it's] invisible, it's a couple of people they know—Berlusconi and his cabinet, maybe. . . . So, what happened to the Gallup poll? Well, I mean, actually, somebody did a database search—one newspaper, the *Christian Science Monitor*, had something about it. It was mentioned in Milwaukee, in a journal. That's it, and that's normal. . . . Right after 9/11, the Bush administration was announcing it's gonna bomb Afghanistan, there was a Gallup poll asking people about that. There was no support for it. They couldn't . . . they didn't publish it. . . . It wasn't published [anywhere] because the story was "everybody supports this." So the fact that almost nobody wants to bomb Afghanistan, you just can't report. And, you know, the most striking fact was the reaction in Latin America. You know, Latin America has a little bit of experience with US power: 2 percent support in Mexico, 4 percent in some other country—basically nobody supported it. Well, you know, that's really important. What it says is that countries that have had a little experience with our benevolence are overwhelmingly opposed to our bombing Afghanistan. But you can't say that because what you have to say is we're noble and we're right. So, that got no publication actually—one small notice in Omaha, that's it. Now, that's what the media are supposed to do; they're serving their purpose. You do not want to tell people our leaders and our intellectual elites despise democracy and we're supported by no one in the world, but we're going to go ahead anyway because we have the power. You don't want to tell people that. So what you tell them is we . . . have humanitarian objectives and we're going to carry out liberation and so on and so forth. And, of course, you don't add to that that Hitler and Mussolini said exactly the same thing. Yeah, they were going to liberate everyone and overcome ethnic cleansing and so on and so forth, and [are] just full of nobility. In fact, . . . there isn't a resort to violence in history—at least that I've been able to find—where the leadership didn't say the same thing. But you don't tell people that. What you tell them is we're doing it because we're angelic and, therefore, support our leaders and march to the beat of the drum and the world is with us except for some crazy Frenchmen and so on—that's basically the story.

ARNO MAYER: There is on the issue of Iraq—and there has been all these last [few] months—an incredible drumbeat of manipulation by the media, of the sort that I think really is incredibly rare and at the same time needs to be explained, though God knows it is difficult to explain . . . the full power and influence of the media and the fact that there are so few genuine dissenting voices that can be heard, whether this be on radio, on television, or in the print media. In my more mischievous moments, I'm inclined to think that Goebbels would be proud or could be proud of the way in which the media in the United States in particular managed to, I would almost say, control channels and, above all, set limits to the kind of discussion that is admissible in this particular moment of the history of this republic.

NOTES

1. *New York Times* Act I

"Fewer people attended than organizers had said they hoped for, even though after days of cold, wet weather, the sun came out this morning. Participants said the shootings in and around the city in the last three weeks had kept people from planning to visit Washington, D.C." Lynette Clemetson, "Thousands March in Washington against Going to War in Iraq," *New York Times*, October 27, 2002.

National Public Radio Act I

Marshall: It was not as large as the organizers of the protest had predicted. They had said there would be 100,000 people here. I'd say there are fewer than 10,000. However, they did accomplish their goal of actually marching around the White House in one continuous stream of people. It is a little bit thin in some areas, but nonetheless, they have marched around the White House. "Profile: Protests against a Possible War in Iraq Taking Place around the Country," *NPR News—All Things Considered,* October 26, 2002.

2. *New York Times* Act II

"The demonstration on Saturday in Washington drew 100,000 by police estimates and 200,000 by organizers', forming a two-mile wall of marchers around the White House. The turnout startled even organizers, who had taken out permits for 20,000 marchers. They expected 30 buses, and were surprised by about 650, coming from as far as Nebraska and Florida." Kate Zemike, "Rally in Washington Is Said to Invigorate the Antiwar Movement," *New York Times,* October 30, 2002.

National Public Radio Act II

"On Saturday October 26th, in a story on the protest in Washington, D.C., against a US war with Iraq, we erroneously reported on *All Things Considered* that the size of the crowd was 'fewer than 10,000.' While Park Service employees gave no official estimate, it is clear that the crowd was substantially larger than that. On Sunday, October 27, we reported on *Weekend Edition* that the crowd estimated by protest organizers was 100,000. We apologize for the error." http://www.npr.org/programs/atc/transcripts/2002/oct/021026.brand.html.

3. "A transitional government headed by a leading businessman replaced President Hugo Chávez today, hours after military officers forced him to resign. It was a sudden end to the turbulent three-year reign of a mercurial strongman elected on promises to distance his country from the United States while uprooting Venezuela's old social order." Juan Forero, "Venezuela's Chief Forced to Resign; Civilian Installed," *New York Times,* April 13, 2002.

"With yesterday's resignation of President Hugo Chávez, Venezuelan democracy is no longer threatened by a would-be dictator. Mr. Chávez, a ruinous demagogue, stepped down after the military intervened and handed power to a respected business leader, Pedro Carmona." "Hugo Chávez Departs," *New York Times,* April 13, 2002.

"In recent days, we expressed our hopes that all parties in Venezuela, but especially the Chavez administration, would act with restraint and show full respect for the peaceful expression of political opinion. We are saddened at the loss of life. We wish to express our solidarity with the Venezuelan people and look forward to working with all democratic forces in Venezuela to ensure the full exercise of democratic rights. The Venezuelan military commendably refused to fire on peaceful demonstrators, and the media valiantly kept the Venezuelan public informed.

Yesterday's events in Venezuela resulted in a transitional government until new elections can be held. Though details are still unclear, undemocratic actions committed or encouraged by the Chavez administration provoked yesterday's crisis in Venezuela. According to the best information available at this time:

Yesterday, hundreds of thousands of Venezuelans gathered peacefully to seek redress of their grievances. The Chavez government attempted to suppress peaceful demonstrations. Chavez supporters, on orders, fired on unarmed, peaceful protestors, resulting in more than 100 wounded or killed. Venezuelan military and police refused orders to fire on peaceful demonstrators and refused to support the government's role in such human rights violations. The government prevented five independent television stations from reporting on events. The results of these provocations are: Chavez resigned the presidency. Before resigning, he dismissed the Vice President and the Cabinet. A transition civilian government has promised early elections.

We have every expectation that this situation will be resolved peacefully and democratically by the Venezuelan people in accord with the principles of the Inter-American Democratic Charter. The essential elements of democracy, which have been weakened in recent months, must be restored fully. We will be consulting with our hemispheric partners, within the framework of the Inter-American Democratic Charter, to assist Venezuela." Philip T. Reeker, deputy spokesperson, US State Department press statement, Washington, D.C., April 12, 2002, available at http://www.state.gov/r/pa/prs/ps/2002/9316.htm.

4. "The disconnect between last Tuesday's monstrous dose of reality and the self-righteous drivel and outright deceptions being peddled by public figures and TV commentators is startling, depressing. The voices licensed to follow the event seem to have joined together in a campaign to infantilize the public. Where is the acknowledgment that this was not a 'cowardly' attack on 'civilization' or 'liberty' or 'humanity' or 'the free world' but an attack on the world's self-proclaimed superpower, undertaken as a consequence of specific American alliances and actions? How many citizens are aware of the ongoing American bombing of Iraq? And if the word 'cowardly' is to be used, it might be more aptly applied to those who kill from beyond the range of retaliation, high in the sky, than to those willing to die themselves in order to kill others. In the matter of courage (a morally neutral virtue): whatever may be said of the perpetrators of Tuesday's slaughter, they were not cowards." Susan Sontag, *New Yorker*, September 24, 2001.

5. "It's an obscene comparison but there was a time in South Africa when people would put flaming tyres around people's necks if they dissented. In some ways, the fear is that you will be necklaced here, you will have a flaming tyre of lack of patriotism put around your neck. It's that fear that keeps journalists from asking the toughest of the tough questions and to continue to bore-in on the tough questions so often. Again, I'm humbled to say I do not except myself from this criticism." Dan Rather (anchor, *CBS Evening News*), available at *BBC Newsnight* on Thursday, 16 May, 2002, http://news.bbc.co.uk/1/hi/programmes/newsnight/1991885.stm.

6. "Look, Seymour Hersh is the closest thing American journalism has to a terrorist, frankly." Richard Perle, former assistant US defense secretary on *CNN Late Edition with Wolf Blitzer*, "Showdown: Iraq," aired March 9, 2003, 12:00 EST.

APPENDIX

FRONT PAGES OF NEWSPAPERS

- America strikes back—TALI-BAM—Afghan terror targets bombed (*New York Post*, October 7, 2001)
- ON THE WAY TO WAR—Aboard the carrier Truman bound for the Persian Gulf (*Daily News*, November 19, 2002)
- US warns Iraq: WE'LL NUKE YOU. Bush: Use WMD at your peril. (*New York Post*, December 11, 2002)
- AXIS OF WEASEL—Germany and France wimp out on Iraq (*New York Post*, January 24, 2003)
- WE WILL PREVAIL—Resolute Bush vows . . . (*Daily News*, January 29, 2003)
- WAR CRY—Bush ties Iraq to terror (*New York Post*, January 29, 2003)
- SADDAM & GOMORRAH [with two subtitles]—US offers him tix to exile [after SADDAM]. TV's millionaire blonde is a bondage babe [after GOMORRAH]. (*Daily News*, January 30, 2003)
- WAR PACT—Bush and Blair tell Saddam: time's up (*New York Post*, February 1, 2003)
- READY TO RUMBLE—Bush & Blair vow no more fooling from Saddam (*Daily News*, February 1, 2003)
- THE GAME IS OVER—Bush warns Saddam (*Daily News*, February 1, 2003)
- PROOF—How Saddam hides terror weapons (*New York Post*, February 6, 2003)
- GAME OVER—Bush gives UN ultimatum on Iraq (*New York Post*, February 7, 2003)
- SACRIFICE [picture shows a cemetery where US soldiers were buried after World War II]—They died for France but France has forgotten (*New York Post*, February 10, 2003)
- TORTURED BY SADDAM—Exclusive: American Gulf War POWs suing Iraq for $900 million (*Daily News*, February 16, 2003)
- FACE OFF [picture shows a New York policeman on a horse kicking a demonstrator during the February 15, 2003, anti-war demonstration]—Scores arrested as anti-war protest strangles Midtown (*New York Post*, February 16, 2003)
- WAR GAMES—Exclusive: Mayor Mike practices handling a terror attack on the City (*Daily News*, February 19, 2003)

- HUNT AND KILL—US plans quick strike on Saddam and his sons (*New York Post,* February 24, 2003)
- FAIR GAME [picture shows cross-hairs over the face of Saddam Hussein]—Bush gives OK to kill him (*Daily News,* February 26, 2003)
- Summit ultimatum—WAR IN DAYS—Bush gives UN last chance to act (*New York Post,* March 17, 2003)
- HERE WE COME—Bush: UN must back war today or else (*Daily News,* March 17, 2003)
- 48 HOURS—President tells Saddam "leave or die" (*New York Post,* March 18, 2003)
- 48 HOURS—Bush gives Saddam deadline to flee (*Daily News,* March 18, 2003)
- DEAD MAN [picture shows Saddam Hussein]—Butcher tells US "come and get me" (*New York Post,* March 19, 2003)
- Bush deadline 8:00 PM—Saddam sneers back: HELL NO, I WON'T GO (*Daily News,* March 19, 2003)
- Special Edition—At 9:33 last night the battle for Iraq began—WAR (*New York Post,* March 20, 2003)
- War special—First strike—GOOD MORNING, BAGHDAD (*Daily News,* March 20, 2003)

MEDIA OWNERSHIP

AOL/Time Warner

Amazon.com (partial)
AOL.com
AOL Europe
AOL Instant Messenger
Cartoon Network
Cartoon Network (Asia/Pacific)
Cartoon Network (Europe)
Cartoon Network (Latin America)
CNN
CNN Airport Network
CNN en Espanol
CNN Headline News
CNN Interactive
CNN International
CNN Newsroom
CNN Radio
Court TV (with Liberty Media)
DC Comics
Entertainment Weekly
Food and Wine magazine
Fortune magazine
Hanna/Barbera Cartoons
HBO
Life magazine
Little, Brown books
MapQuest.com
Money magazine
Netscape Communications
Netscape Netcenter
New York 1 News

People magazine
Radio stations (too many to list)
Road Runner
TBS Superstation
Time magazine
Time Warner Book Group (UK)
Time Warner Cable
Travel and Leisure magazine
Turner Adventure Learning
Turner Classic Movies
Turner Home Satellite
Turner Network Television
  (TNT)
Turner Network Television
  (Asia/Pacific)
Warner Books
Warner Faith
Warner Brothers International
  Theaters
Warner Brothers Studios
Warner Channel (Latin America,
  Asia-Pacific, Australia,
  Germany)
Warner Home Video
WB Television Network

Disney
A&E Television (37.5 percent,
  with Hearst and GE)
ABC.com
ABCNews.com
ABC Television Network
Buena Vista Home Video
Buena Vista International
Buena Vista Music Group
Buena Vista Television
Caravan Pictures
Disney Channel
Disney.com
Disney Cruise Line
Disney Institute

Disneyland, Anaheim, CA
Disneyland Paris
Disney MGM Studios
Disney Regional Entertainment
Disney's Animal Kingdom
Disney Vacation Club
E! Entertainment (with Comcast
  and Liberty Media)
ESPN (80 percent—Hearst
  Corporation owns the
  remaining 20 percent)
ESPN2
ESPN Extreme
ESPN News
ESPN Now
ESPN.sportzone.com
Family.com
Go Network
History Channel (with Hearst
  and GE)
Hollywood Pictures
Hollywood Records
Lyric Street Records
Mammoth Records
Miramax Films
Mr. Showbiz
NASCAR.com
NBA.com
Oscar.com
Radio stations (too many to list)
SoapNet
Tokyo Disneyland (partial)
Toon Disney
Touchstone Pictures
Touchstone Television
Toysmart.com
Walt Disney Pictures
Walt Disney Records
Walt Disney Television
Walt Disney Theatrical
  Productions

Walt Disney World, Orlando,
FL
Walt Disney World Sports
Complex

General Electric
Bravo
CNBC
Universal Pictures
GE Aircraft Engines
GE Commercial Finance
GE Consumer Products
GE Industrial Systems
GE Insurance
GE Medical Systems
GE Plastics
GE Power Systems
GE Specialty Materials
GE Transportation Systems
MSNBC
NBC
Sci-Fi
Telemundo

News Corporation
Advertiser (Australia)
Australian (Australia)
Courier-Mail (Australia)
Daily Telegraph (Australia)
Fiji Times (Australia)
Fox Movie Channel
Fox News Channel
Fox Television
Gold Coast Bulletin (Australia)
HarperCollins books
Herald Sun (Australia)
Mercury (Australia)
National Geographic Channel

News International (UK)
News of the World (UK)
Newsphotos (Australia)
Newstext (Australia)
New York Post
NT News (Australia)
Post-Courier (Australia)
Sky Television
Sun (UK)
Sunday Herald Sun (Australia)
Sunday Mail (Australia)
Sunday Tasmanian (Australia)
Sunday Telegraph (Australia)
Sunday Territorian (Australia)
Sunday Times (Australia)
Sunday Times (UK)
The Times (UK)
20th Century Fox
Weekly Standard
Weekly Times (Australia)

Viacom
BET
CBS
MTV
Paramount Home
    Entertainment
Paramount Pictures
Radio stations (too many to list)
Showtime Channel
Simon and Schuster Adult
    Publishing Group
Simon and Schuster Children's
    Publishing
Simon and Schuster New Media
Sundance Channel

Source: Columbia Journalism Review, available at http://www.cjr.org/tools/
owners

Brooklyn, New York, September 14, 2001

US troops during Operation Iraqi Freedom

"War, Peace, and Patriotism": Protesters, Soldiers, and Chicken Hawks

The master class has always declared the wars; the subject class has always fought the battles. The master class has had all to gain and nothing to lose, while the subject class has had nothing to gain and all to lose—especially their lives.

—Eugene Victor Debs

GEORGE W. BUSH (State of the Union speech, January 29, 2003): Tonight I have a message for the men and women who will keep the peace, members of the American Armed Forces: Many of you are assembling in or near the Middle East, and some crucial hours may lay ahead. In those hours, the success of our cause will depend on you. Your training has prepared you. Your honor will guide you. You believe in America, and America believes in you.

The following two veterans were interviewed in Washington, D.C., during the anti-war demonstration on October 26, 2002.

VETERAN 1: War is not the answer. It is not a rational way to react.

VETERAN 2: Because I am an ex–army officer and I don't think that wars solve any problems.

DAVID CLINE: Well, war is when humans resort . . . descend to barbarism. It's when we go back to barbarism. And . . . and, in the end, war is men, and today, it's also women, but it's men going out there, from two different sides just trying to kill each other.

In the time I was in Vietnam, I was a combat infantryman, a rifleman, and, sometimes, had to be a machine-gunner. In the time that I was in Vietnam, I was wounded. I got shot and when I got shot, my left lung collapsed and I was reported dead, but I was sent to the hospital. Forty-five days later, I was released from the hospital and two weeks after that, I was sent back out in "the bush," we call it, to go back out and fight. I was wounded again when a piece of shrapnel hit my shoulder. That was a minor wound, and . . . and then I was sent back out in the field and then I got shot a third time. I got shot in the right knee on December 20th, 1967. About 2:00 in the morning, we were overrun . . . by North Vietnamese regulars near the Cambodian border and I was wounded there. And, so I have three Purple Hearts for three wounds received in combat. I have a Brown Star for bravery. [A] combat infantry badge . . . and I'm disabled from my wounds.

There hasn't been a war on American soil, so most people in America don't know what war is really about. For people that are in the military and fighting wars, they are permanently changed sometimes for the better, but oftentimes for the worst by war. People are wounded physically, people are killed, people are wounded mentally, emotionally, psychologically. People are contaminated with military toxins.

In Vietnam . . . they used Agent Orange. They sprayed Agent Orange over about 1/5th of South Vietnam. They were killing the . . . the idea was they were going to kill the bushes and kill the crops so that the Viet Cong couldn't get no food and they had no place to hide. In fact, it didn't have any effect on that. But what it did was it killed a lot of the farmland and it killed a lot of the jungle and it contaminated a lot of people, including large numbers of American G.I.s . . . some people say over a quarter-million G.I.s. At that time, many thousands of veterans died because what we were getting was cancers. A lot of people were getting cancers, various . . . soft-tissue sarcomas, leukemias; some people had birth-defected children. A lot of people developed a condition called chloracne, which was a permanent skin rash.

So, for people who serve in war, war is hell. Now in America and in a lot of the West today, there's been these movies that sort of turn war into games, you know. And that's part of the problem with our culture today . . . war and killing has been turned into an entertainment. The real deal is not like what they show you. The real deal is like, where you're damaged for life from war.

Donald Rumsfeld made comments recently, talking about the draft; when Charles Rangel asked him to re-introduce the draft and Rumsfeld said, "The draft was the people that got sucked in when they couldn't get out and they were of no use." You know, like the 18,000 Americans [who] died in Vietnam were draftees. Out of the 58,000, 18,000 of them were draftees. He says they were of no use. To me, as a Vietnam combat veteran, they were brothers we lost. You know, when I hear a guy saying that, it gets me sick.

MICHAEL FOLEY: The draft had been in place since really not long after the Second World War; [in] 1947 they brought it back. And because there were so many people who were draft age during that period, they came up with this system of deferments that allowed people out of the drafts in various ways, and these were supposed to be in activities that were in the nation's interest. So, you could get a draft deferment if you were going to college or if you worked for a company that was doing something supposedly in the nation's interest. All the famous politicians today who managed to escape it—most of them did it; all of them I guess did it legally.

DAVID CLINE: Well, we call them "Chicken Hawks." When they could have gone to fight in their youth, they avoided it, and now that they're in charge, they're going to send other people's youth to fight. They're the hawks, but they were the chickens when it was their turn. So we call them "Chicken Hawks." You got George Bush, he was in the Texas National Guard. Now, you've got to remember, during the Vietnam era, the National Guard in Texas was a place to get out of the draft, it was a way to dodge the draft, if you had the money and the connections. See, 'cause that was the name of the game, then. If you had the money, you could get out. If you didn't, you'd get sent to the war.

EMILY REINHARDT: In Bush's case, he leapfrogged over a hundred thousand people to get into the Texas National Air Guard. And even when he was in the National Guard, he was AWOL [absent without leave] for a month. You know, he didn't take his duties in that seriously either and that was a way to get out of serving and he wasn't serious about it. It makes you sad to think that this man is president and he couldn't take anything seriously in his youth.

GREG PALAST: He thought we should fight in Vietnam. Bill Clinton didn't want to go to Vietnam because he didn't believe in the war. That's legitimate. That's ideological. But Bush believed that other guys should go to the war; but you know, he was just your typical spineless, yellow, gutless coward who was afraid of bullets and I don't blame him. I don't blame him. But

Chickenhawks sign at the anti-war demonstration in New York,
February 15, 2003

it's the cowards who are always ready to send other guys to war and his entire Cabinet is filled with chicken hawks.

MICHAEL FOLEY: The draft system was therefore incredibly unfair because it basically guaranteed that middle- and upper-class people, young men, were more likely to escape the draft, while working-class, poor, and minority men were more likely to be drafted and sent into the military.

> *I can never forgive a leadership that said, in effect: These young men— poorer, less educated, less privileged—are expendable (someone described them as "economic cannon fodder") but the rest are too good to risk. I am angry that so many of the sons of the powerful and well placed . . . managed to wangle slots in Reserve and National Guard units.*
>
> —Colin Powell, *My American Journey*

MICHAEL FOLEY: There were illegal ways to get out of the draft too, which included leaving the country. We don't know how many exactly left, but somewhere between thirty and fifty thousand went to Canada or Mexico or somewhere else. And then there became in 1967 a national movement of people who openly defied the draft—a movement of civil disobedience in which they would get together in cities around the country and have draft card turn-ins, where they would turn in their draft card, which that alone was a crime. You had to have the draft card on you at all times. So, if you turned it in and sent it to the Justice Department in Washington, you were breaking the law. So the idea was that if they had enough people do this, they could undermine the way that the draft worked and hopefully undermine the war. That didn't really work out the way they'd hoped, but it did have the effect [of] finally making the Johnson administration pay attention to the anti-war movement.

US NATIONAL ANTHEM

> Then conquer we must,
> when our cause it is just,
> And this be our motto:
> "In God is our trust."
> And the star-spangled banner
> in triumph shall wave
> O'er the land of the free
> and the home of the brave
> —"The Star-Spangled Banner"

DAVID CLINE: I have to say that, as a disabled American combat veteran, I get offended when I hear that, that we're unpatriotic. Today, those who are fighting against what George Bush and his crew are doing are patriots. For them to call us unpatriotic is to make the word "patriotism" devoid of meaning. Patriotism is not getting in line behind the president, saluting the president, dying for the credibility of the president. Nor is it just putting up a flag and waving that in mindless nationalism. Patriotism is the love of your country and is the love of the world today.

LESLIE CAGAN: People identify with the flag. After 9/11 the flag just showed up every place. Certainly here in New York you couldn't walk two steps without seeing an American flag.

KATHA POLLITT: In America, the flag, the piece of cloth, the emblem, represents something that it does not represent in many other countries. In America, the flag is the . . . it's the civic deity.

DREAD SCOTT: My most well-known work is a work called "What's the Proper Way to Display a US Flag?" which I made in 1988, and in 1989 it became the center of national controversy over its use of the American flag.

The work had a photomontage on the wall which consisted of text, which said, "What's the Proper Way to Display a US Flag?" on it. Below that were South Korean students burning US flags, holding signs that said, "Yankee, go home, son of a bitch," and below that were flag-draped coffins coming home on a troop transport from Vietnam. Below that, on the wall, was a shelf that held books [where] people could write responses to the question "What's the Proper Way to Display a US Flag?" and below that was a flag that people had the option of standing on, if they wanted to. There were laws passed at the city, state, and federal level which ended up outlawing the work. The US Senate voted unanimously to condemn the work as they passed the legislation to protect the flag so that people could not desecrate the US flag. And the president of the United States at that time, George Bush 1st, publicly denounced me as well. But there was a tremendous amount of support for the work. If you went to the housing projects, or the ghettos or barrios—[people] waited on line . . . to see the work; . . . they waited for an hour. There were a lot of people who thought that the work was speaking at least to them, if not for them. There was a very interesting comment from a German woman who said: "If Germans carried on about the flag the way the people in the US do, they'd be called fascists again." And she thought that would be right.

There was a person, who was a poor black woman, who wrote that the police had shot her brother and then they kicked over his body to make sure the "nigger was dead." And that cop wore a flag patch on his arm as many cops do, or most cops in most of the police departments do. And so that's how it kind of impacts people most directly. There are a lot of people who know the history of this country and its present-day reality, from the genocide of the native people to the enslavements of Africans to the rulings on the *Dred Scott* original Supreme Court case in 1853 where the Supreme Court ruled that there're no rights that a black person has that a white man is bound to respect and you know, that Court flew a flag on it . . . the flag that was on the bombs that destroyed Hiroshima and Nagasaki and killed many civilians there. This flag has meant nothing more than murder and plunder for the vast majority of the people in the world. And a lot of people who have been given the opportunity to debate this question have very insightful comments about it.

There is no flag large enough to cover the shame of killing innocent people.
—Howard Zinn

DAVID CLINE: I always say that veterans are treated like a condom, "Use once and throw away." Because, you know, we have a cadence we sing, "If they tell you to go, there is something you should know: They wave the flag when you attack. When you come home, they turn their back."

EDWARD DANIELS II: I came back and I was in fatigues and I came off the plane, you know, and I felt hey, you know, this is a good feeling. I'm going to be welcome as a hero. . . . You know, the thing I really wanted was a nice piece of American apple pie and a glass of milk. And so I go into the base cafeteria and I got me a nice glass, a tall glass of milk and a piece of apple pie and I was eating and there was this black guy, came along; works in the base cafeteria and was cleaning up, taking trays and dishes off and putting them . . . and he said to me, he came over to my table and he said, "Oh, you're one of those guys. You just came back from . . . you know, right." And so I think I'm ready to get some praise. So I fix my jacket, my fatigue shirt. And he says, "You're one of them fools."

There was no welcome. And the majority of time you kept it to yourself. To tell you what honestly happened when I came back—I was so disillusioned. I didn't have any . . . I didn't feel very good about it because most people weren't considerate enough to have an understanding of the position that we as the soldiers were put in as pawns to fight something that we were led to believe [was] for an altruistic purpose, and it wasn't. And so, I gave away all of my military stuff; you know, the jungle fatigues . . . and the only thing I kept was the boots because they were very good, you know, I'm being honest. The boots were very good. You know, I kept the jungle boots and I gave away everything else. I mean, I didn't want to know. The only [thing] I wanted to [do] was to get an education, get some benefits, and go on with my life.

DAVID CLINE: War veterans come home, suffering from a lot of bad memories, bad dreams, nightmares, inability to react with other people normally 'cause they have a lot of feelings of anger and guilt and a lot of people begin to self-medicate—drugs, but, mainly, alcohol.

EDWARD DANIELS II: You have trouble sleeping at night, you have an erratic sleep pattern and you're always looking for some kind of crutch to get you through. You know, and it's a mind-boggling thing because you always say to yourself, "I'll never be the same person I was, that I was before I got into this." You know, God's honest truth, I always said to myself, "I wish that I could be myself, that I was before I went into the military." And reality is, it ain't going to happen. We shouldn't be used as a scapegoat because it wasn't our decision to make. And we didn't format policy. We didn't implement policy. And we certainly weren't in a position to do anything about it. You know, most of us came from impoverished backgrounds and things of that nature. If most of us probably could've gotten a better grip on when we were coming up out of school, an honest appraisal, an honest teaching from our teachers, I think we'd [have] been a little more open-minded and receptive to the different information that was coming. It wasn't done. It wasn't done. We were greatly disserviced.

DAVID CLINE: They're more interested in throwing *their* money into building new weapons and making new bombs and going after somebody else, 'cause this is the direction that we're getting from our country.

Then, periodically, they'll come to you later on and pat you on the back and say, "You served your country. Now, come out here and march for the next generation to go off and fight." See, that's what we're about— we changed that. In Vietnam, we came back . . . we helped start the "Vietnam Veterans Against the War." We said, "No, you're not going to just keep using one generation of veterans to send off another generation." That's what started this whole "Veterans for Peace Movement," it's that these are veterans who have been there and done that and now we're saying that we've got to stop that.

ASIF: I coordinate a program called "Roots," which stands for "Revolution Out of Truth and Struggle." And "Roots" is a program that focuses on issues of militarism as it impacts those most under siege of militarism. So, when we talk about militarism and specifically military recruitment, which communities are being impacted? Well, usually it's an economic issue, and it's also heavily saturated with issues of race and ethnicity. . . . So, the people who are most directly targeted are people from Black, Latino, poor Asian, as well as Native American communities. So, these are the communities that we are most concerned with as well in doing our counter-military recruitment work.

So, we have a campaign currently against the Junior Reserve Officer Training Corps, which is a military program targeting so-called inner cities, areas which are dilapidated, which are plagued with all kinds of drugs and guns, and our people in those communities often resort to the military or military institutions as a way out. And so JROTC uses valuable school funds to get young people of color into the military, and each year 40 percent of the military's recruits, overall military recruits, comes out of the JROTC, the Junior Reserve Officer Training Corps.

The spirit of this country is totally adverse to a large military force.
—Thomas Jefferson, 3rd US president (1801–1809)

WILLIAM HARTUNG: Our military budget . . . is now almost $400 billion a year; just the increase that they got after September 11th of close to $50 billion is bigger than the entire military budget of any other country in the world. We're spending more, apparently, than the next twenty-five or twenty-six countries combined. [See Appendix.] But because Bush is also pushing large tax cuts, because he's also increasing the Homeland Security budget, and much of that money goes to the same companies for security and military kinds of items, because they've had big supplemental requests to pay for the war in Afghanistan [and] the war in Iraq, which could cost several hundred billion dollars . . . there's not much left in the US budget for domestic needs. More than 50 cents on the dollar is already going to the military. And that is going to increase once we have the tax cuts, once we pay for these wars. Bush's budget deficits are now pushing $400 billion a year—the largest in the history of our country.

LARRY HOLMES (speaking at the House of the Lord Church in Brooklyn, New York, November 21, 2002): They are going to spend billions of dollars on this war, an occupation—how many we don't even know. At a time when they are closing senior-citizen centers right here in Brooklyn, throwing senior people out, they can't even have their meal, "meals on wheels," or whatever. And they're going to raise the tuition at CUNY [City University of New York] and push the students out. And all the services for the homeless have been shut down and all they're doing with the homeless now is arresting them. And at the same time all this money is being wasted . . . on murder! This is a crime!

REV. AL SHARPTON (speaking at the Riverside Church, New York City, December 8, 2002): What George Bush has done is he's told America to ignore what they ought to be awakened to, because the bogeyman is coming. Don't worry about prescription drugs, the bogeyman's coming. Don't worry about affordable housing, the bogeyman's coming. Don't worry about rising hunger, the bogeyman's coming. Don't worry about deficits in the states and the cities, the bogeyman's coming. We can't even keep schools up to where they ought to be in this present technology. But we can get billions of dollars to go after the bogeyman.

MICHAEL RATNER: Right now, there's a tremendous opposition to the war. There's a rising tide. It's in small communities, it's in big communities, it's in churches, it's in hospitals, it's in workplaces, it's everywhere now. And one part of that aspect is to get city councils in cities throughout the United States to pass resolutions opposed to the war. And you might say,

"Well, what do they have to do with the foreign policy of the United States?" Well, those city councils have to meet the budgets for their cities.

WILLIAM PERKINS: We [New York residents] are suffering from a fiscal crisis of over $3 billion of budget. And we need our police, we need our hospitals, we need our senior centers, we need our schools. New York City has joined 140 other such cities by passing Resolution 549A, and thus we 8 million New Yorkers have joined many, many other Americans in saying that we want peace, not war. [See Appendix.]

REV. AL SHARPTON (speaking at the January 18, 2003, anti-war demonstration in Washington, DC): Dr. King challenged that the money in Vietnam could be used here to build housing for the homeless and the care for children. We argue that you say you have no money for state deficits. You have no money for childcare. You have no money for uninsured grandmothers. But you have 100 billion to 1 trillion dollars to go to Iraq about weapons that you can't find. We can't back up. You won't fight in our name.

LESLIE CAGAN: This country has a long history, especially since World War II, of constantly relying on militarism and its military strength to "solve problems." And we know that doesn't really solve the problems, it just adds another layer to the problems. It may suppress a set of problems, or a group of people, but it doesn't really deal with the fundamental reasons why people around the world may be unhappy with us or the way we are interacting with their countries. And over and over again, our country has relied on force. From Vietnam to Grenada and Panama, Nicaragua, we didn't send our troops, so we funded the Contras, and all over the world the US really has developed to be the military superpower in the world. I think a simple way of saying it is that it is good for business. . . . You know, it is sort of ironic that it was Dwight D. Eisenhower, a president of this country, and indeed a general of this country, who came up with the phrase "the military industrial complex." Anytime there is a war, there is a greater investment, an even greater investment in military operations.

WILLIAM HARTUNG: [They are] using Iraq as a big cash machine to give contracts to companies tied to President Bush who are then going to recycle some of that money and give it to his re-election. He's running this government the way Suharto ran Indonesia. You know, it's crony capitalism. It's taking care of his friends. It's actually worse than what Eisenhower warned about; the military industrial complex. It's . . . almost like we have this little military junta in Washington that's pretending we have a democracy. But when it comes to any important decision, it's made by the

Pentagon, it's made by the security officials. They're preempting our civil liberties. They're elbowing the State Department out of the way. They're insulting our allies. This is not what democracy is supposed to be about. And so, I think, that's really the threat. It's . . . not just the money. It's the militarization of American culture and politics. Thankfully, I think, people are not going to sit still for that.

NELSON MANDELA (speaking at the International Women's Forum in Johannesburg, South Africa, January 30, 2003): What I'm condemning is that one power, with a president who has no foresight, who cannot think properly, is now wanting to plunge the world into a holocaust. And I'm happy that the people of the world, especially those of the United States of America, are standing up and opposing their own president.

ANGELA DAVIS (speaking at the February 15, 2003, anti-war demonstration in New York City): Good afternoon. This is a good afternoon to be in New York City. This vast community gathered here in fierce solidarity with people who are demonstrating all over the world—in Seattle, and in Raleigh, in Rome, London, Cape Town, and Manila—this community most perfectly represents the City of New York. Thank you. . . . We are here to challenge the Bush administration's strategy of pretending to defend democracy by trampling upon people's democratic rights. . . . The Bush administration tries to generate fear and hysteria—tactics reminiscent of the McCarthy era. . . . Some people may have joined that march of fear, but many more are participating in demonstrations of collective courage. We are here today because we are concerned about the deterioration of political culture instigated by George W. Bush. He has lowered the level of political discourse to discussions about evil-doers and hunts for terrorists. This simplistic political discourse is fundamentalist in impulse. It is designed to stop critical thinking. It is designed to prevent us from recognizing . . . US government and corporate designs on Iraq's oil. Our responsibility to stop the war on Iraq is a responsibility to the future. We cannot allow the US government to establish a precedent that justifies future assaults, especially on peoples of the southern region of the world. We are here because we are concerned about rising poverty in our own country. We are concerned about attacks against single mothers, about structural racism, about homophobia, about the incarceration of what the government considers disposable population. . . . We are here because we stand together in solidarity with the September Eleventh Families for Peaceful Tomorrows, and we are heartened because we know that our bodies, our voices, our hearts do make a difference. They make a difference

[when] we unite as we are doing today—when we unite for peace and when we unite for justice. Thank you.

PHYLLIS BENNIS (speaking at the February 15, 2003, anti-war demonstration in New York City): It's George Bush that is isolated in the world. It's not us. We are the American people. We are part of a global movement. We are building a new internationalism with the United Nations as a part saying "no to war." The people of the world are saying "no to war."

CROWD: The world says no to war. The world says no to war. . . .

OSSIE DAVIS (speaking at the February 15, 2003, anti-war demonstration in New York City): My pleasure now is to bring you one of God's choicest children, Archbishop Desmond Tutu!

ARCHBISHOP DESMOND TUTU (speaking at the February 15, 2003, anti-war demonstration in New York City): Hello. Hello. You're all such wonderful, wonderful people. I want to give you a very warm clap. . . . Join me in clapping . . . you. Come on!

President Bush, listen to the voice of the people, for many times the voice of the people is the voice of God. Vox populi, vox dei. Listen to the voice of the people saying, "Give peace a chance. Give peace a chance." And let's say it once more so that they can hear in the Pentagon, so that they can hear in the White House. What do we say to war? *The crowd replies* (NO). What do we say to peace? *The crowd replies* (YES). Yeah!

GEORGE W. BUSH (in four different speeches):

May God bless America.

And may God continue to bless the United States of America.

Good night and may God continue to bless America.

May God bless our country and all who defend her.

CHESHIRE FRAGER: The idea that God takes sides is absurd. I think if God takes sides it is the side of the suffering.

ROSEMARIE PACE: Yesterday, for example here in New York, we had a rally that was led by an interfaith religious leaders' forum, and it was a wonderful example of people coming together from Judaism, from Islam, from Christianity, from Buddhism.

CHESHIRE FRAGER: You can't talk about anything of justice being involved in a war. There is nothing of justice involved with war.

REV. PETER LAARMAN: A war of aggression of this kind cannot be justified according to any religious principle.

REV. AL SHARPTON (speaking at the Riverside Church, New York City, December 8, 2002): April 4th, 1967, Martin Luther King Jr. stood here in this historic pulpit and said why he had to oppose the war in Vietnam.

MARTIN LUTHER KING III (speaking at the February 15, 2003, anti-war demonstration in New York City): Today, thirty-six years later, we are on the brink of going to war. And the reality is you do not stop terrorism by terrorizing others. For he said, my father, that darkness cannot put out darkness, only light can put out darkness. He said that violence cannot stamp out violence, only nonviolence can stamp out violence.

REV. JESSE JACKSON (speaking at the January 18, 2003, anti-war demonstration in Washington, DC): Dr. King said what made America right was the right to fight for the right. We march today, and we vote. Isaiah said, "Let's start war no more and beat their swords into plowshares, and their spears into pruning-hooks." Don't let them whip your spirits. Don't let them discredit you. Don't let them dissuade you. Here we stand—red, yellow, brown, black, and white. We are precious in God's sight. This is America at its best.

REV. AL SHARPTON (speaking at the January 18, 2003, anti-war demonstration in Washington, DC): If Dr. King was here to celebrate his birthday, Mr. Bush, he would not be inside preparing for military buildup. He'd be outside saying give peace a chance. So as I leave you, I wish you a Happy King Day. Happy birthday, Martin. We haven't dropped the banner. Happy birthday, Martin. We're going to still stand for peace. Happy birthday, Martin. Just like Bush's son is in the White House, your children are in Washington today. We will stand up. We will not back down. . . .

HOWARD ZINN: Well, this has been a remarkable peace movement in the United States. The movement against the war in Vietnam was the greatest peace movement we ever had in the United States. . . . [Before the Vietnam war] we never had a peace movement in the United States that actually had an effect on the policy makers, that help[ed] to stop a war. But that's what happened during Vietnam. What has happened now is even more surprising because it took several years for the peace movement to develop during the Vietnam War. You know, 1965, 1966, a very small peace movement; 1967, '68, it began to grow. [But] here, we have had a peace movement growing very, very fast even before the war begins. That has never happened before. Peace activity, peace protests, vigils, teach-ins, demonstrations. We've never had that happen in very small towns around the United States. That's what's happening now. We have, you know, little towns like Missoula in Montana, you know—probably a lot of people don't even know where Montana is. Montana is a state that has very few people in it. Its towns are very small, but there have been demonstrations in little towns in Montana, little towns all over the country. This has never happened before. And, we've never had such a sign of support for the anti-war movement in the arts, in the theater, in the movies, in the music world. During the Vietnam War, Jane Fonda became famous. Jane Fonda was a symbol of artistic resistance. But beyond Jane Fonda, there wasn't a lot of anti-war activity. Now, hundreds of Hollywood stars have signed petitions against the war. Rock musicians have taken out full-page ads in the *New York Times* against the war. It's quite unusual, quite different. So, we have this unusual juxtaposition, and that is, on the one hand, we have an administration which seems to be totally determined to go to war, more so than at any other point in American history; [never before] has there been such an absolute fixation on war. At the same time, we have the quickest growth of an anti-war movement that we've ever had in American history.

NOAM CHOMSKY: Even the *New York Times*, which tries to play this kind of thing down, they had a front page story. . . . It said, ". . . there may still be two super-powers on the planet: the United States and world public opinion" [February 17, 2003; see next page]. Now, of course, when they say "the United States," they mean the US government, not the population, so the correct statement is "There are two superpowers on the planet—one, Washington, which has all the guns, and one, world public opinion including quite a lot of the United States."

GEORGE W. BUSH (Cincinnati Museum Center speech, October 7, 2002): Tonight I want to take a few minutes to discuss a great threat to peace. The threat from Iraq stands alone because it gathers the most serious dangers of our age in one place. It possesses and produces chemical and biological weapons. It is seeking nuclear weapons.

EMILY REINHARDT: The "Threat to Peace" poster—we did it in the centerfold of one of our issues originally. We just thought it'd be interesting to see what America has in regards to that: how many war criminals we hide; how many, you know, weapons we have; how many nuclear sites . . . anything [in] regards to how we terrorize the rest of the world.

CURT GOERING: Over the last decade as the number of armed conflicts has increased around the world, Amnesty's work has taken place increasingly in the context of armed conflict. Because this is the time when human rights violations increasingly . . . or violations of the laws of war [are being committed]. So, the world context has taken Amnesty into the situation. So, we have begun now to monitor how wars are conducted. . . . We've done it in the former Yugoslavia during the Kosovo War. And we're very critical of certain types of behavior in terms of how the wars were conducted; the flying of planes at high altitudes where the [pilots] weren't able to . . . distinguish between soldiers and civilians.

REED BRODY: You know, war is no longer two armies fighting it out from trench to trench. In modern wars unfortunately 90 percent of the casualties are civilians. We see that in civil wars, but we also see it in international wars—so any war is going to have a devastating impact on civilian populations.

A New Power In the Streets

A Message to Bush Not to Rush to War

By PATRICK E. TYLER

WASHINGTON, Feb. 16 — The fracturing of the Western alliance over Iraq and the huge antiwar demonstrations around the world this weekend are reminders that there may still be two superpowers on the planet: the United States and world public opinion.

News Analysis

In his campaign to disarm Iraq, by war if necessary, President Bush appears to be eyeball to eyeball with a tenacious new adversary: millions of people who flooded the streets of New York and dozens of other world cities to say they are against war based on the evidence at hand.

Mr. Bush's advisers are telling him to ignore them and forge ahead, as are some leading pro-war Republicans. Senator John McCain, for one,

New York Times, February 17, 2003

> *It is my conviction that killing under the cloak of war is nothing but an act of murder.*
>
> —Albert Einstein

GEORGE W. BUSH (press conference, March 6, 2003): Our goal is peace, for our nation, for our friends and allies, for the people of the Middle East.

NELSON MANDELA (speaking at the International Women's Forum in Johannesburg, South Africa, January 30, 2003): If there is a country that has committed unspeakable atrocities in the world, it is the United States of America. They don't care, they don't care for human beings. Fifty-seven years ago, when Japan was retreating on all fronts, they decided to drop the atom bomb on Hiroshima and Nagasaki. Killed a lot of innocent people who are still suffering from the effects of those bombs. Those bombs were not aimed against the Japanese. They were aimed against the Soviet Union to say, "Look, this is the power that we have. If you dare oppose what we do, this is what is going to happen to you."

SETSUKO NAKAMURA THURLOW (speaking at the West Park Presbyterian Church in New York City, December 1, 2002): On August 6th, 1945, I was a 13-year-old grade 8 student. At 8:15 I saw outside the window the bluish white flash like a magnesium flare. I remember the sensation of floating in the air. As I regained consciousness in the total darkness and silence I realized I was pinned in the ruins of the collapsed building. By the time I came out of the building it was on fire. That meant about thirty of my classmates who were in the same room were burnt to death alive. I turned and saw the outside war. Although it was morning it looked like twilight because of the dust, smoke, and particles in the air. People at a distance saw the rising mushroom cloud and heard the thunders roar. I did not see the cloud because I was in it. I did not hear the roar, just the deadly silence broken only by the groans of the injured.

APPENDIX

ANNUAL MILITARY BUDGETS

$379 billion (2003)	United States*
$34.8 billion (2001)	United Kingdom
$29 billion (2000)	Russia
$27 billion (2000)	France
$23.1 billion (2001)	Germany
$18.7 billion (2000)	Saudi Arabia
$15.9 billion (2000)	India
$14.5 billion (2000)	China
$12.8 billion (2000)	South Korea
$12.8 billion (2000)	Taiwan
$7.5 billion (2000)	Iran
$3.3 billion (2000)	Pakistan
$1.8 billion (2000)	Syria
$1.4 billion (1999)	Iraq
$1.3 billion (2000)	North Korea
$1.3 billion (2000)	Yugoslavia
$1.2 billion (2000)	Libya
$425 million (2000)	Sudan
$31 million (2000)	Cuba

*$48 billion increase from Fiscal Year 2002 to Fiscal Year 2003
Source: Adapted from International Institute for Strategic Studies, *The Military Balance 2000–2001.*

CITY AND COUNTY COUNCIL AND RELATED RESOLUTIONS OPPOSING PREEMPTIVE/UNILATERAL WAR IN IRAQ

California
Alameda
Arcata
Berkeley
Cotati
Culver City

Davis
El Cerrito
Emeryville
Fairfax
Ft. Bragg
Los Angeles

Malibu
Mendocino County
Oakland
Palo Alto
Point Arena
San Fernando
San Francisco
San Jose
San Luis Obispo
Santa Barbara
Santa Clara County
Santa Cruz
Santa Monica
Sebastopol
Topanga
Ukiah
West Hollywood

Colorado
Boulder
Crested Butte
Denver
Nederland
Pitkin County
Ridgway
San Miguel County
Silver Plume
Telluride

Connecticut
Cornwall
Kent
Mansfield
New Haven
New London
Salisbury

Florida
Key West

Georgia
Atlanta

Hawaii
State House of Representatives
Kauai County

Idaho
Blaine County

Illinois
Chicago
DeKalb
Evanston
Oak Park
Park Forest
Urbana

Indiana
Bloomington
Gary

Iowa
Des Moines
Iowa City (Mayoral proclamation)

Maine
State Senate
State House
Bar Harbor
Hallowell
Isle au Haut
Orono
Portland
Waterville

Maryland
Baltimore
Garrett Park
Glen Echo
Greenbelt*
Mount Rainier

Takoma Park
Washington Grove

Massachusetts
Amherst
Boston*
Brookline
Cambridge
Greenfield
Leverett
Lincoln
Northhampton
Pittsfield
Provincetown
Somerville
Wendell
Williamstown

Michigan
Ann Arbor
Brown Township
Detroit
Ferndale
Hamtramck
Kalamazoo
Lansing
Manistee County
Pleasanton Township
Saginaw
Traverse City

Minnesota
St. Paul

New Hampshire
Hanover (opposing pre-emptive
    war, passed May 13, 2003)

New Jersey
East Orange
Englewood
Irvington

Jersey City
Lambertville
Maplewood
Montclair
Newark
Paterson
Plainfield
Princeton Borough
Prospect Park
Roosevelt

New Mexico
Santa Fe

New York
Buffalo
Danby
Greenburgh
Ithaca
Mount Vernon
New Paltz
New York City
Nyack
Plattsburgh
Rochester
Rockland County
Rosendale
Syracuse
Tompkins County
Woodstock

North Carolina
Carrboro
Chapel Hill
Orange County

Ohio
Akron
Belmont County
Cleveland
Cleveland Heights

Dayton
East Cleveland
Garfield Heights
Lorain
Lorain County
Oberlin
Shaker Heights

Oregon
Corvallis
Eugene*
Lincoln City
Multnomah County
West Linn

Pennsylvania
Philadelphia
Pittsburgh
Wilkinsburg
York

Rhode Island
Bristol
Providence

Texas
Austin

Utah
Springdale

Vermont passed March 1, 2005
Bethel
Brattleboro
Burlington
Cabot
Calais
Cavendish
Dummerston
East Montpelier
Fayston

Greensboro
Guilford
Hinesburg
Huntington
Jamaica
Jericho
Johnson
Marlboro
Marshfield
Middlebury
Middletown Springs
Monkton
Montgomery
Montpelier
Moretown
Ripton
Rochester
Rockingham
Roxbury
Salisbury
Sharon
Strafford
Thetford
Tinmouth
Waitsfield
Warren
Weathersfield
Westford
Westminster
Weybidge
Wheelock
Windham
Worcester
Woodbury

Virginia
Alexandria
Charlottesville

Washington

San Juan County
Seattle*
Tacoma
Vashon Maury Island
    Community Council

Washington, DC

Wisconsin

Dane County
Madison
Milwaukee
Shorewood Hills
Stevens Point

*In some cases, council rules or consensus prevented a resolution. In those cases, councils have often drafted a letter to the president and their representatives in Washington, D.C., in lieu of a resolution. Letters listed here were signed by a majority of the city's council members.

Also, the National Black Caucus of Local Elected Officials, a caucus of the National League of Cities, made a resolution supporting peace.

Source: Cities for Peace, A Project of the Institute for Policies Studies, available at http://www.ips-dc.org/citiesforpeace

> *In these several hundred wars against communism, terrorism, drugs, or sometimes nothing much, between Pearl Harbor and Tuesday 11 September 2001, we always struck the first blow.*
>
> —Gore Vidal

Table IV.1. US Military Operations, 1948–2000

Berlin Airlift	Berlin	1948/1949
Korean War	Korea	1950/1953
Taiwan Straits	Taiwan Straits	1954/1955
Suez Crisis	Egypt	1956/1956
Blue Bat	Lebanon	1958/1958
Taiwan Straits	Taiwan Straits	1958/1959
Taiwan Straits	Quemoy/Matsu Islands	1958/1963
Congo	Congo	1960/1962
Laos	Laos	1961/1962
Berlin	Berlin	1961/1963
Vietnam War	Vietnam	1962/1973
Operation Ranch Hand	Vietnam	1962/1971

Table IV.1. US Military Operations, 1948–2000 (continued)

Operation Rolling Thunder	Vietnam	1965/1968
Operation Arc Light	Southeast Asia	1965/1970
Operation Freedom Train	North Vietnam	1972
Operation Pocket Money	North Vietnam	1972
Operation Linebaker I	North Vietnam	1972
Operation Linebaker II	North Vietnam	1972
Operation Endsweep	North Vietnam	1972/1973
Operation Kingpin	North Vietnam	1970
Operation Tailwind	Laos	1970
Cuban Missile Crisis	Cuba/Worldwide	1962/1963
(None)	Chinese Nuclear Facilities	1963/1964
Red Dragon	Congo	1964
Powerpack	Dominican Republic	1965/1966
Chase	Various	1967/1970
Six Day War	Mideast	1967/1967
Red Fox	Korea theater	1968/1969
Graphic Hand	USA Domestic	1970
Red Hat	Johnston Island	1971
Garden Plot	USA Domestic	1972
Nickel Grass	Mideast	1973
Eagle Pull	Cambodia	1975
Frequent Wind	Evacuation of Saigon	1975
New Life	Vietnam	1975
Mayaguez	Cambodia	1975
Tree Incident	Korea	1976
Setcon I	Colorado	1978
Ogaden Crisis	Somalia/Ethiopia	1978
Red Bean	Zaire	1978
Yemen	Iran/Yemen/Indian Ocean	1978/1979
Elf One	Saudi Arabia	1979/1989
Rok Park Succession Crisis	Korea	1979/1980
Eagle Claw/Desert One	Iran	1980
Setcon II	Colorado	1980
Creek Sentry	Poland	1980/1981
Central America	El Salvador/Nicaragua	1981/1992
RMT (Rocky Mtn. Transfer)	Colorado	1981

Table IV.1. US Military Operations, 1948–2000 (continued)

Gulf of Sidra	Libya/Mediterranean	1981
Bright Star	Egypt	1981
US Multinational Force	Lebanon	1982/1987
Early Call	Egypt/Sudan	1983
Arid Farmer	Chad/Sudan	1983
Urgent Fury	Grenada	1983
Intense Look	Red Sea/Gulf of Suez	1984
Achille Lauro	Mediterranean	1985
Attain Document	Libya	1986
El Dorado Canyon	Libya	1986
Blast Furnace	Bolivia	1986
Praying Mantis	Persian Gulf	1988
Ernest Will	Persian Gulf	1987/1990
Nimrod Dancer	Panama	1989
Just Cause	Panama	1989/1990
Promote Liberty	Panama	1990
Hawkeye	St. Croix, US Virgin Islands	1989
Classic Resolve	Philippines	1989
Sharp Edge	Liberia	1990/1991
Steel Box/Golden Python	Johnston Island	1990
Desert Shield	Southwest Asia	1990/1991
Imminent Thunder	Southwest Asia	1990
Proven Force	Southwest Asia	1991
Desert Storm	Southwest Asia	1991
Desert Sword	Southwest Asia	1991
Desert Calm	Southwest Asia	1991/1992
Desert Farewell	Southwest Asia	1992
Eastern Exit	Somalia	1991
Productive Effort/Sea Angel	Bangladesh	1991
Fiery Vigil	Philippines	1991
Victor Squared	Haiti	1991
Quick Lift	Zaire	1991
GTMO	Haiti/Guantanamo, Cuba	1991
Safe Harbor	Haiti/Guantanamo, Cuba	1992
Silver Anvil	Sierra Leone	1992
Garden Plot	Los Angeles, California	1992

Table IV.1. US Military Operations, 1948–2000 (continued)

Provide Transition	Angola	1992
Provide Relief	Somalia	1992
(none)	Liberia	1992
Restore Hope	Somalia	1992/1993
Continue Hope	Somalia	1993
Korean Nuclear Crisis	North Korea	1993/1994
Distant Runner	Rwanda	1994
Sea Signal	Haiti/Guantanamo, Cuba	1994/1996
Safe Haven/Safe Passage	Cuba/Panama	1994/1995
Taiwan Straits	Taiwan Strait	1995/1996
Zorro II	Mexico	1995/1996
Assured Response	Liberia	1996
Quick Response	Central African Republic	1996
Guardian Assistance	Zaire/Rwanda/Uganda	1996
Assurance	Zaire/Rwanda/Uganda	1996
Silver Wake	Albania	1997
Guardian Retrieval	Congo (formerly Zaire)	1997
Noble Obelisk	Sierra Leone	1997
Bevel Edge	Cambodia	1997
Noble Response	Kenya	1998
(none)	Asmara, Eritrea	1998
Shepherd Venture	Guinea/Bissau	1998
Infinite Reach	Sudan/Afghanistan	1998
Strong Support	Central America	1998/1999
Avid Response	Turkey	1999
Stabilize	Timor	1999
Fundamental Response	Venezuela	1999/2000
Silent Promise	Mozambique/South Africa	2000
Agathe Path	Puerto Rico	1989/?
Enhanced Ops	Puerto Rico	?/Present
Support Justice	South America	1991/1994
Steady State	South America	1994/1996
Green Clover	South America	199?
Laser Strike	South America	1996/?
Constant Vigil	Bolivia	199?
Ghost Zone	Bolivia	1990/1993?

Table IV.1. US Military Operations, 1948–2000 (continued)

Wipeout	Hawaii	1990/Present
Greensweep	California	1990
Grizzly	California	1990/Present?
Ghost Dancer	Oregon	1990/Present?
Badge	Kentucky	1990/Present?
Selva Verde	Colombia	1995/Present
Coronet Nighthawk	Central/South America	1991/Present
Coronet Oak	Central/South America	1977/1999
Provide Hope I	Former Soviet Union	1992
Provide Hope II	Former Soviet Union	1992
Provide Hope III	Former Soviet Union	1993?
Provide Hope IV	Former Soviet Union	1994
Provide Hope V	Former Soviet Union	1998/1999
Alliance	US Southern border	1986/Present
Golden Pheasant	Honduras	1988/Present
Safeguard	Arizona	1995/Present
Hold-the-Line	Texas	1995/Present
Gatekeeper	California	1995/Present
Resolute Response	Africa	1998/Present
Monuc [UN PKO]	Congo	2000/Present
Sierra Leone	Sierra Leone	2000
New Horizons	Central America	Present
Korea	Korea	Present
Desert Falcon	Saudi Arabia	1991/Present
Southern Watch	Southwest Asia/Iraq	1991/Present
Provide Comfort	Kurdistan	1991/1994
Provide Comfort II	Kurdistan	1991/1996
Northern Watch	Kurdistan	1996/Present
Pacific Haven/Quick Transit	Iraq/Guam	1996
Iris Gold	South West Asia	1993/Present
Vigilant Warrior	Kuwait	1994
Vigilant Sentinel	Kuwait	1995/1997
Intrinsic Action	Kuwait	1995/1999
Desert Spring	Kuwait	1999/Present
Desert Focus	Saudi Arabia	1996/Present
Phoenix Scorpion I	Iraq	1997

Table IV.1. US Military Operations, 1948–2000 (continued)

Phoenix Scorpion II	Iraq	1998
Phoenix Scorpion III	Iraq	1998
Phoenix Scorpion IV	Iraq	1998
Shining Presence	Israel	1998
[none](air strike)	Iraq	1993
[none] (cruise missile strike)	Iraq	1993
Desert Strike	Iraq	1996
Desert Thunder	Iraq	1998
Desert Fox	Iraq	1998
Provide Promise	Bosnia	1992/1996
Maritime Monitor	Adriatic Sea	1992
Maritime Guard	Adriatic Sea	1992/1993
Sharp Guard	Adriatic Sea	1993/1995
Decisive Enhancement	Adriatic Sea	1995/1996
Determined Guard	Adriatic Sea	1996/Present
Sky Monitor	Bosnia-Herzegovina	1992/Present
Deny Flight	Bosnia-Herzegovina	1993/1995
Decisive Endeavor	Bosnia-Herzegovina	1996
Decisive Guard	Bosnia-Herzegovina	1996/1998
Deliberate Forge	Bosnia-Herzegovina	1998/Present
Able Sentry	Serbia-Macedonia	1994/Present
Nomad Vigil	Albania	1995/1996
Nomad Endeavor	Taszar, Hungary	1996/Present
Quick Lift	Croatia	1995
Deliberate Force	Bosnian Serbs	1995
Determined Effort	Bosnia-Herzegovina	1995
Joint Endeavor	Bosnia-Herzegovina	1995/1996
Joint Guard	Bosnia-Herzegovina	1996/1998
Joint Forge	Bosnia-Herzegovina	1998/Present
Determined Falcon	Kosovo/Albania	1998
Eagle Eye	Kosovo	1998/1999
Shining Hope	Kosovo	1999
Sustain Hope/Allied Harbour	Kosovo	1999

Table IV.1. US Military Operations, 1948–2000 (continued)

Provide Refuge	Kosovo	1999
Open Arms	Kosovo	1999
Allied Force/Noble Anvil	Kosovo	1999
Determined Force	Kosovo	1998/1999
Cobalt Flash	Kosovo	1999
Joint Guardian	Kosovo	1999/?

Source: Federation of American Scientists, available online at GlobalSecurity.org.

Human Rights Day, December 10, 2002, UN Headquarters, New York

V

"Civilization": Targeting Iraq

I think it would be a good idea.
—Mahatma Gandhi (when asked what he thought
about Western civilization)

VICTORIA DE GRAZIA: It's probably better known, the story of the British attitudes toward Arabs through Egypt. I mean, it was often said that the Egyptians were good for nothing but to help dig in archaeological sites. There was always toward the Middle East efforts on the part of the British, particularly, to classify and to diminish the Arabs with respect to each other. So, it was a history of high-handedness, and if you want enormous disrespect based on fear . . . the British in proportion to their fear of the locals developed more elaborate racist ideas.

I do not admit . . . that a great wrong has been done to the Red Indians of America, or the black people of Australia . . . by the fact that a stronger race, a higher-grade race . . . has come in and taken its place.
—Winston Churchill to the Palestine Royal Commission, 1937

VICTORIA DE GRAZIA: We have much documentation about the attitudes of major leaders like Churchill whose racism was well known toward the Arabs. It was also well known toward the Indians and particularly to the figure of Gandhi.

A half-naked fakir [who] ought to be laid, bound hand and foot, at the
gates of Delhi and then trampled on by an enormous elephant with the
new viceroy seated on its back.
                                                              —Winston Churchill

VICTORIA DE GRAZIA: It was the justification for not allowing the self-
rule—[the notion] that they were too backward to make it possible. But
again, this is the legitimization of the fact that it was known that the Iraqi
areas represented a very evolved area of the Ottoman Empire. But it was
always true that the most evolved areas, first Egypt and then the area of
Mesopotamia, were treated as backward. But the backwardness was in a
large measure a result of the pressures and the way these areas were divided, re-divided, ruled by colonial powers.

ZAINAB BAHRANI: Ancient Mesopotamia is so important in terms of archae-
ology and history because it is considered to be the world's first urbanized
culture—the world's first civilization where people started to build cities. It's
the place where writing was invented, where the wheel was used for the first
time. It's the place where we have the earliest use of monumental architec-
ture, the earliest literature, poetry, scientific text, mathematics—all of these
occurred first in Mesopotamia. The people who were the first to use writing are called the Sumerians. They had control over the south of Iraq from
the 4th to the end of the 3rd millennium B.C. After that time we have the
Babylonians coming. The most famous Babylonian king is Hammurabi of
Babylon, whose law code is known to all schoolchildren. Babylon was the
most important city in the 2nd millennium B.C., but by about 1000 B.C.
the north of Iraq becomes important. And we have the rise of the Assyrian
Empire. They were very learned people. They had libraries. They had
schools. They had very educated elite with all sorts of texts that survive on
astronomy, the sciences, medicine. The reason that the ancient
Mesopotamian civilization is so important is that many, many aspects of
our own culture today in the West actually derive from the practices of the
ancient Assyrians and the Babylonians and even the ancient Sumerians. So,
much of that written knowledge trickled down or was borrowed from the
Babylonians and the Assyrians through to the Greeks and the Romans, and
then from the Greeks and the Romans down to our own time.

    Another period in time in which Iraq's history is very important is
the Abbasid Medieval period of Islamic history. So, we're talking about a
period between the 8th and the 10th Centuries A.D., when Baghdad was
the capital, when Baghdad was the center of the Islamic world. The caliphs
of Baghdad were very interested in knowledges of all sorts, and this was the

time when universities were built. The oldest university was built in Baghdad in 1000 A.D. This was the time when all of the ancient Greek texts—the things that were written by Plato and Aristotle and all of the famous Greek classical writers that we know of and admire today—these texts were copied down, were translated into Arabic, and were kept in libraries and archives in Medieval Baghdad, whereas, in the West, nobody cared about them. And if not for that preservation and translation movement of the Abbasid caliphs, all of that magnificent knowledge of the ancient Greeks would be lost to us today.

VICTORIA DE GRAZIA: United States policy in Iraq today has to be seen [as] a two-century-long history of great pressure exercised by the Western great powers in the Middle East. That was the main zone of contention: re-division of imperial spoils. The European great powers have been involved at least since the time of Napoleon to push back the Ottoman Empire, to dissolve it. So, starting with 1878 with the pressure and then the colonization of Egypt, taking it away from the Ottoman Empire and then continuing with the conflicts, Germany, France, Italy over North Africa, concluding with the seizure of Libya in 1912. So, the Great War—World War I—was seen very clearly in all sorts of secret accords as being the moment in which this entire area would be in effect taken away and re-colonized by the Western powers. Already during the war the Sykes-Picot [agreement was in place; see Appendix] two administrative entrepreneurs representing the French and the British had signed an agreement, a secret agreement, which provided that at the end of the war the area where Iraq now exists was going to be divided. That is, the French were going to take Syria and Lebanon, and the British would take the area of these great provinces extending through the Tigris and Euphrates, which is present-day Iraq. And with the war ended [this secret agreement]—although denounced publicly [and] publicized by Lenin, to the great distress of the allies as well as the Russians, who counted on taking part in this despoiling of the Ottoman Empire—this proceeded. When the Arabs found out about it at the Versailles, though they had expected their freedom and had even supported the allies in the effort to get that freedom, there was terrible distress. And when it was indeed found out they would not be liberated as they expected, there was this great uprising in 1920 which the British put down in their area with enormous violence. Violence which, given the techniques of the time and technologies of the time, [was] in many respects similar to that exercised by the United States in the first Gulf War and then in the second Gulf War as well—enormous superiority of arms. There was talk about using poisoned gas . . . there was a slaughter of thousands and thousands of Iraqis.

I do not understand the squeamishness about the use of gas. I am strongly in favour of using poisonous gas against uncivilised tribes.

—Winston Churchill, 1919

VICTORIA DE GRAZIA: Now, that was the area out of which Iraq was created, which was considered to be the most advanced area of the Mideast. And it was the area which was most irregularly divided up, which is to say that Iraq, the new state that was emerging, was prevented from having access to the Persian Gulf by the creation of this mini-state of Kuwait, and it was protested from the very outset. It was expected that the state of Kurdistan would be created. But that was prevented by the *parcelization* of the Kurds partly into a new Persian state, partly into the state of Iraq, partly into the emerging state of Turkey, which was given, therefore, a greater shape. So, it was a birth that was in many ways monstrous. The British would stay in Iraq constantly because it was a source of constant rebellion against this status quo—an area where there was this constant protest against this enormous abuse of power as it was viewed from the moment of the Versailles when it was discovered that the freedom for peoples spoken about by Wilson . . . the notion that there would be a just peace that would free particularly the Arabs, who were led to believe they would be supported by the British. . . . This delusion was such that there would be constant history, then, of enormous rebelliousness and animosity and particularly around the state of Iraq.

40 YEARS LATER . . .

TIMOTHY MITCHELL: Saddam Hussein first came to attention in 1963. In 1963 the government of Iraq was overthrown with the assistance of the United States that brought to power the Baath Party. Saddam Hussein was a junior activist in the Baath Party. That party stayed in power only briefly but came back into power in 1968, in the meantime . . . having killed off many of the democratic opponents who have been in power before that. Saddam then re-emerges in 1968, when the Baath seizes his power again. And he essentially is number two in the regime, from 1968 for the first decade through to 1979. He is very much the strong man behind the scene. He is organizing the party operators, he is organizing the security operators, he is also organizing the oil industry and taking control of the resources of the oil industry and putting them in the hands of the party and into himself. After Saddam Hussein becomes the president in 1979, he begins to consolidate his control on power. And that happens to coincide with the Islamic revolution in Iran.

There has been a history of conflicts between those two regimes, Iran and Iraq, and the dispute over territories in the south. Saddam Hussein decides to take advantage of the weakness of Iran in the aftermath of the revolution and invades his neighbor. Officially the United States is neutral in the Iran-Iraq War, and officially it supports UN resolutions embargoing onto both sides. Behind the scenes, however, it begins to do two things: First, it supports Saddam Hussein; secondly, and at the same time, it also supports and allows channeling of funds to the other side in the war as well, to Iran. The US support of Saddam Hussein begins very early on and becomes more significant with time. Because [the US] doesn't want this support to be public, it mostly goes through third parties—through allies such as Egypt for the supply of arms, to allies such as Saudi Arabia [and] Kuwait—for help to finance the war.

GREG PALAST: We have a president going completely berserk over Saddam Hussein's pieces of nuclear weapon. Who gave it to him? The Saudi Arabians—[this] is our information and we're confident of it—gave Saddam Hussein 7 billion dollars to build an atomic bomb. They pulled it out before he could finish it, but they still gave him 7 billion dollars. And they could not do that without the US government's support. That was during the Reagan and Bush administration in the 1980s, when we were happy to use Saddam Hussein to contain Iran.

TIMOTHY MITCHELL: The direct US assistance takes the form particularly of intelligence information which they share with the Iraq regime, particularly two years into the war—around 1983, 1984—when the Iranians begin to recover from the initial attack and turn around and start to threaten Iraq more directly. From early on in the war, and particularly from that moment once the Iranians begin to take the offensive, we now know that the Iraq forces turned to the use of chemical weapons. While the Iraq regime was using those chemical weapons, to the knowledge of the international community, the United States went on supporting [Saddam Hussein] and even helping him in the use, because what the US was doing most directly was giving him the battlefield information about the arrangement of Iranian forces against whom the Iraqis were using chemical weapons. There were subsequent occasions in which they were used, including the better-known one later on toward the end of the war. He turned on to re-conquer the north part of the country, the Kurdish part of the country, and used chemical weapons again—this time, against the Iraqis themselves, against the Kurds in the north.

GREG PALAST: We were giving a wink and a nod to allow Saddam Hussein to use chemical weapons if he so chose. Not only the Kurds were affected, were attacked, but . . . the Marsh Arabs around Basra were also attacked and that didn't bother us at all. It didn't bother America at all that both sides were chewing up people and poisoning them.

TIMOTHY MITCHELL: In the later part of the war, one other important form of support was direct financial aid to supply food aid for Iraq, which again helped to continue to pursue the war against Iran. The United States also gave diplomatic support to Iraq in the Iran-Iraq War—in particular, insisting that the attempts by the UN to bring an end to the war [were] carried out in a way that was favorable to the Iraq government. Specifically, the US blocked the attempt by the UN to impose a settlement that would name Iraq as the aggressor in the war. The significance of that is that if Iraq was named as the aggressor it will be liable for reparation—for paying financial compensations to Iran at the end of the war. At the end of the Iran-Iraq War, [in] 1988–1989, the US at that time was very keen to establish closer ties with Iraq. [It] called Saddam Hussein a force for moderation in the region, was a little bit uncomfortable about his attack on the Kurds, but with that behind him the US was looking for closer ties. Saddam Hussein and the Iraq government now had to dispute with another neighbor, dispute with the neighbor [to] the south, Kuwait. It was a dispute [over] two things—oil, a share of oil fields between the two countries, and also about financial issues: Kuwait had subsidized the war for Iraq and was now demanding the repayment of those debts, and Iraq was in very severe economic straits after the war, needed funds for its own rebuilding, and considered those demands unreasonable.

GREG PALAST: The US ambassador Glasby told Saddam Hussein that the Bush administration had no problem if he attacked Kuwait. However, the deal was he was only supposed to attack their oil fields on the border areas because Kuwait was illegally stealing Iraqi oil. What they were doing is that they were drilling into a common pool of oil while the Iraqis could not because their system had been destroyed by the Iranians. The joint production agreement that they had was being violated. Now, George Bush, the daddy, our first Bush president is an oil man, as is his son. If you break your agreements in an oil field, you get punished. And so, he told Saddam, "Go punish those guys." What Saddam did is that he said, "Oh, listen, moving in ten miles is easy. Let's go the rest of the way."

TIMOTHY MITCHELL: The United States told Iraq that it had no particular position on its dispute with Kuwait, and the Iraq regime seems to have interpreted that as giving them a free hand to threaten Kuwait as they see fit. What they actually did is invaded Kuwait in August of 1990. In fact, the US was not happy about that, and that was the moment in which the relations suddenly changed.

RAMSEY CLARK (speaking at the House of the Lord Church in Brooklyn, New York, November 21, 2002): When we unleashed the attack on Iraq on January 16th, 1991, for forty-two days, there were aerial sorties attacking the people of Iraq. The Pentagon claims 110,000 aerial sorties by US aircraft. One every thirty seconds, every minute of every hour of every day, for forty-two days—88,500 tons of bombs. That's what the Pentagon tells us. It is the equivalent of seven and a half Hiroshimas. It killed . . . estimates vary: one former secretary of the Navy said at least 200,000. Colin Powell, who you want so much to respect, was asked during the assaults, "How many Iraqis do you think you've killed?" and he said: "Frankly that's not a question I am very interested in."

VICTOR SIDEL: The Iraq War, war against Iraq, in 1991 produced thousands, tens of thousands, of military casualties, as well as civilian casualties. In some ways, even more important, the aftermath of the war, the destruction of the power supplies, the destruction of hospitals, other kinds of damage in Iraq, led to a vast amount of disease and disability and led to deaths among civilians in the succeeding years.[1]

ROGER NORMAND: I helped organize the first fact-finding mission to Iraq three weeks after the Gulf War—the first Gulf War in 1991. What we found is that, contrary to the public image here in the United States of a clean war . . . the US led coalition, by targeting the infrastructure, particularly the electricity, had caused a massive humanitarian crisis. The chain of events was: Attack the electricity, water and sanitation. Iraq is a modern country, 70 percent urban, which means that suddenly the population which was used to getting clean water in taps at home had to scavenge for water, dirty water. And given the war and given the collapse of the public health system, you had a huge increase in disease and death due to simple diarrhea, which hadn't happened for years in Iraq—[involving] mostly children, of course, because children are most vulnerable to diarrheal disease. So, what we found after the first war was over 100,000 civilian casualties, deaths, mostly as a result of disease, not [from] being hit by bombs, and mostly children, not soldiers or adults. It was clearly not an attack against Iraqi military. It was an attack against Iraqi economy, which meant civilians suffered the most. And, in fact, this is a war crime because under international law the two most important principles are that you must always only hit military targets, never civilian targets. And we saw many civilian targets that were hit systematically, not by accident. And the second principle of international law is that, even if you hit a legitimate military target, you can't have excessive civilian casualties. And that means that when you hit something like electricity, which should not even be a legitimate military target, but when you hit electricity and you cause tens of thousands, well over a hundred thousand deaths, mostly among children, clearly that's disproportionate. And so, clearly, that was a violation of the laws of war.

RAMSEY CLARK (speaking at the House of the Lord Church in Brooklyn, New York, November 21, 2002): We imposed sanctions first on August 6th, which is Hiroshima day, in 1990. And we blocked medicine and we blocked food, as absolutely as we humanly could, until 1997. UNICEF, a hope for children still, despite everything, reported in August of '91, that there were 47,500 children identified dead as a result of the sanctions. The food and agriculture organization [FAO], if we really looked at [it], could eliminate hunger, could eliminate malnutrition, something we ought to think about seriously and do.... [It] reported in October of 1996, 575,000 children under the age of 5 have died as a direct result of manufactured and forced impoverishment and deprivation of needed food, needed medicine, needed healthcare treatment—dead because of that.

I think this is a very hard choice, but the price—we think the price is worth it.
— US ambassador to the UN Madeleine Albright, May 12, 1996

NORMAN SOLOMON: I thought about Madeleine Albright when I went to the Al-Mansour Children's Hospital in Baghdad. I thought about her interview on the CBS program *60 Minutes* in 1996, when at that point she was the US ambassador to the United Nations, soon to become the US secretary of state. And the network correspondent, Leslie Stahl, asked her about the UN estimate of 500,000 children who had been already dead, who had already passed away because of the US-led sanctions on Iraq. And Madeleine Albright's response was, Yes, this is very troubling but, and this is a direct quote from Mrs. Albright, ". . . we think it's worth it." And so it's clear that in the minds of elites—and, you know, you have to look at Tony Blair in Britain or Berlusconi in Italy, other leaders of countries that became accomplices to this crime of war—a calculation has been present very similar to the one that Madeleine Albright enunciated. "We think it's worth it"; you know, "We're willing to lead the sanctions. We're willing to drop the 2,000-pound bombs, send the cruise missiles, because we have decided it's worthwhile."

VICTOR SIDEL: There're estimates by UNICEF, by other international agencies, that hundreds of thousands of children, perhaps as many as 500,000 children, were directly affected by the sanctions, by the aftermath of the Gulf War, and therefore suffered, many of them dying, over the course of this period because of malnutrition, because of lack of medical care, because of disease.

ROGER NORMAND: We were the first group to do surveys, public health surveys, and show that half a million children, this was in 1996, had died as a result of sanctions. This is from increased mortality rates—again, due to the fact that not only was the infrastructure destroyed in the 1991 war, but sanctions prevented the full rebuilding of the infrastructure. And of course under sanctions you had a marginal economy; people couldn't work, people didn't have an income, had enormous inflation. What you had actually, it was really quite incredible and unprecedented in history, the United Nations was presiding over the systematic impoverishment of an entire nation. And so, whereas Iraq previously was a fairly wealthy country, with a strong middle class, by the end of sanctions, certainly by '95–'96, which was before the first Oil for Food program was instituted, you had incredible poverty. You had hunger and starvation in a country sitting on top of black gold.

JACQUELINE SOOHEN: Many children had to work on the street. There's a lot of poverty. They were used to a very high standard of living, very educated, and all of a sudden they were put in this incredibly demeaning position. They had their faces just stuck in the mud over and over and over again.

HANNY MEGALLY: As a human rights organization we take the view that sanctions are also a tool of war. And during wartime there are rules that are applied. And the sanctions are not an exception to that, and one has to look at the limits to the use of power. In a wartime situation one looks at the prohibitions that safeguard civilians—and during a war, civilians are not supposed to be targeted deliberately.

JOSE ALVAREZ: Some people said that the sanctions were intended to create pain on a population so that they would revolt and topple Saddam Hussein. This particular approach has a real problem if you don't think revolt is actually politically viable. It also is, of course, quite inhumane to the extent that it imposes huge humanitarian costs, as apparently it has;

whether it is prompted by the sanctions or by the cynical manipulations of the sanctions by Saddam Hussein, the result is still the same.

ROGER NORMAND: And so at that point you have the Oil for Food deal, which was not meant to end sanctions. It was not even meant to restore the Iraqi people to their previous position. In a sense it was pain management. It was making the sanctions a little bit better. It did increase the nutritional status of Iraq and Iraqi children. But you still have a tremendous mortality rate. So when UNICEF did their survey, a nationwide survey in 1998, they confirmed what we had found, which was more than a doubling of child mortality, and the figures again were more than 500,000 excess deaths.[2]

GEORGE W. BUSH (press conference, March 6, 2003): If war is upon us because Saddam Hussein has made that choice, we would have the best equipment available for our troops, the best planes available for victory, and we will respect innocent lives in Iraq.

WILLIAM HARTUNG: Since the first Gulf War, there's kind of a new American way of warfare which focuses on aerial bombardment, precision munitions. In the case of the cluster bomb, it's a bomb which contains many small bomblets, sometimes 100 or 200, which can spread over an area of several hundred yards. So that means if you're trying to take out concentrated troops, you can kill and injure many troops. But it also means if you drop it in a civilian area, you could hit many civilians. And many of these little bomblets remain unexploded on the ground. So, for example, in Afghanistan the canisters were yellow—the same color as the food packets that they were dropping. And kids would pick these things up because they are small. It looks like a toy. And they would lose their arms. They would be killed. Human Rights Watch and other groups have said that these weapons should be banned because they are indiscriminate.

CURT GOERING: And they have a relatively high dud rate, or unexploded rate; they don't explode when they hit. So, for those cluster bombs that don't explode, they are in effect landmines. And they've fallen in people's gardens, in their backyards. We've seen many cases in Iraq where unexploded cluster bombs have later exploded when children have picked them up, and sometimes whole families have been decimated by these cluster bombs.

WILLIAM HARTUNG: We haven't heard as much about the extent of depleted uranium. And that can be used for artillery shells, for some of the bombs that are dropped from attack planes like the A-10. Some of the helicopters can also fire these shells. And they're also used to shield the tanks—as armor for the tanks. And what was learned after that war was that although the uranium is depleted . . . it's not highly enriched like it would be for a bomb . . . it still has very negative health effects. And once you explode something with depleted uranium and you spread the dust all over an area, people breathe it; soldiers are in closed quarters and the tanks [are] exposed to it. It's believed that it contributes to a lot of the illnesses that have been seen both among Iraqis and among veterans of that war.

DAVID CLINE: Gulf War veterans . . . Gulf War veterans came home and they've been sick all along and have been fighting to get recognition. You know, right now, today, there were 607,000 G.I.s, men and women . . . servicemen and -women, who served during Desert Storm. Today, over 226,000 of them are disabled, according to the VA [Department of Veterans Affairs]. That's 36 percent, and that's not counting the people that they turned away. You know, during Desert Storm, they said, "Oh, we hardly lost anyone—293 people were killed." I think that was the number—293. Today, it's over 10,000. Ten thousand two hundred and thirty-four people are dead that were Desert Storm soldiers, according to the VA, from military contamination, from depleted uranium, from the PB pills, from those anthrax shots—from a lot of things.

CURT GOERING: Depleted uranium is another concern of Amnesty International . . . since the heavy use in earlier wars. The concerns of the long-term, maybe even short-term medical effects of depleted uranium— the dust that's inhaled or the areas around where they've been used.

JACQUELINE SOOHEN: You could walk into any single hospital in Basra, and not only was it completely filthy and there was complete lack of equipment and complete lack of drugs, but the wards were simply . . . the children's wards, especially, were just crowded, crowded with kids who were suffering from leukemia, who were suffering from tumors, and they had absolutely no chance of survival. The doctors were very, very blunt. We'd meet a child and they would say, "This child has one week" or "This child has one month to live." And this happened over and over again over the course of the time we were in Iraq. I saw a couple of children who literally died in front of me. And it was almost even more heartbreaking to meet a child, to have a conversation with them, to learn about them, meet their family and come back a week later, come back a month later, and they were dead. And the other effect of that was that . . . I spent a lot of time with the women in Iraq and a lot of time with the women in Basra. And women were . . . when they could carry a pregnancy to term, they were always afraid. But a lot of the time, women would simply try to avoid having children. They would try to avoid getting pregnant because they were so afraid [about] what their children would look like because [of] the horrible pictures that you would see of children with no faces, with no organs, with organs outside; those are real. The congenital deformities that have been the result of depleted uranium are real, and people are really afraid.

ZAINAB BAHRANI: During the 1991 Gulf War, some damages did occur to important sites. There was the Ziggurat of Ur in the south of Iraq where there were bomb craters found around it. . . . The southernmost site of the Ziggurat was damaged, although it remains standing. The arch of the capital city of Ctesiphone was cracked and is in danger of collapsing at any minute. A few minarets from the Middle Ages were toppled because of bombs that went astray. Several mosques of the Middle Ages received some damage. Some museums were hit. And then after the war was over, all the museums were looted and about 5,000—between 4,000 and 5,000 objects—were looted from museum collections and archaeological sites and appeared for sale in the Western antiquities market.

> *The images you are seeing on television, you are seeing over and over and over. It is the same picture of some person walking out of some building with a vase and you see it twenty times. And you think, my goodness, were there that many vases? Is it possible that there were that many vases in the whole country?*
>
> —Defense Secretary Donald Rumsfeld, April 11, 2003

ZAINAB BAHRANI: No repairs could be made in the aftermath of the war because the Iraqi government at that time requested . . . UNESCO to send teams of international scholars to survey the sites to assess the damages and to bring materials to rebuild and to protect these ancient sites. UNESCO did take the proposal to the United Nations twice, and it was twice vetoed by the United States and Great Britain. During the 1991 war, there was a great deal of damage. But I imagine that this war will result in an even much larger amount of damage, especially given the campaign that they have called the "shock and awe" campaign over Baghdad. So, that really doesn't leave much to be hoped for—especially for the medieval standing monuments, the ancient university, the Mustansaria that dates to 1233, the Abbasid Palace from 1179. I imagine that monuments like that will have fallen, will have been destroyed. One of the places under attack right now is the city of Karbalah in the south of Iraq. And I think that many people in the West don't realize that for the Shiite Muslims, this is the holiest site anywhere. It's a pilgrimage site, and Muslims come from all over the world to visit it. And if the mosques there are damaged or destroyed, it would really be like destroying St. Peter's in Rome, and I think Muslims everywhere would be incredibly outraged.

THE VOICES

JACQUELINE SOOHEN: Also the children are incredibly afraid. Even from the bombings in 1998 and 1999, and the continued bombing in the no-fly zone in the south [has] really traumatized kids. Some of them stopped speaking. A lot of them, they can't relax like normal children would relax, and . . . the closer the war came and the more they heard about it, the more you could see the fear in their eyes. And they just talked about the voices of the bombs and how scared they were of the voices.

JESSICA LANGE (speaking at the January 18, 2003, anti-war demonstration in Washington, DC): To all of you who came here from around this country. To all that are here in spirit across the world, who join together in this quest for peace to send a message—to send a message that the path this

Anti-war demonstration in Washington, DC, October 26, 2002

administration is on is wrong and we object in our hearts, in our minds. It is an immoral war that they are beginning, and we must not be silenced. We have to be able to stand up and say No. We are the people. You are not speaking for us.

DANNY GLOVER (speaking at the February 15, 2003, anti-war demonstration in New York City): We stand here because our right to dissent and our right to be participant have been hijacked by an administration of liars and murderers who curse us because we stand in the way of their tyranny, who curse us because we stand in the way of their unholy and brutal agenda. An administration whose felony and greed is insatiable. We stand at this threshold of history and say to them: "Not in our names! Not in our names!"

SUSAN SARANDON (speaking at the February 15, 2003, anti-war demonstration in New York City): And as Eleanor Roosevelt said, "It isn't enough to talk about peace. One must believe in it. It isn't enough to believe in it. One must work at it." And we here today are working at it.

HARRY BELAFONTE (speaking at the February 15, 2003, anti-war demonstration in New York City): This is not the first time that we as a people have been misled by the leadership. We were misled by those who created the falseness of the Bay of Tonkin, which falsely led us into a war with Vietnam—a war that we could not and did not win. We lied to the American people about Grenada and what was going on in that tiny island. We lied to the American people about Nicaragua, El Salvador, Cuba, and many places in the world. And we stand here today to let those people and others know that America is a vast and diverse country. And we are part of the greater truth of what makes our nation.

PHYLLIS BENNIS (interviewed during the February 15, 2003, anti-war demonstration in New York City): I just came from the United Nations. I just met with Kofi Annan, and we told him that there are people now in 660 cities around the world today that are marching saying "no to war" and that we're looking to the UN to take the lead. And it's very important that we see the UN as a context for this anti-war mobilization.

SCOTT RITTER: The British and American governments were supposed to put forward a resolution today, which basically authorizes the use of military force by the Security Council. They were forced to withdraw this resolution because of what the French and the Russians and Chinese did yesterday, and what billions of people did today. So, I'm hopeful. We bought a month; the next meeting of the Security Council will be on March 14th, and I'm hopeful that there will be the ability of those who oppose this war to continue to rise up and expand their numbers so that there's no way President Bush can ever think about waging war with Iraq and try and pretend that it somehow has the mandate of the people.

VICTOR SIDEL: Just before the large demonstrations that took place in New York City in mid-February, both the International Physicians for Prevention of Nuclear War and the International Association of Lawyers conducted a press conference at the United Nations' New York City site. And at that press conference, IPPNW introduced a letter that had been sent to Kofi Annan, the secretary general of the United Nations, and a letter to President Bush, calling on the United Nations Security Council not to permit an attack on Iraq, and calling on the United States not to conduct an attack on Iraq.[3]

NOTES

1. Iraqi deaths directly attributable to the (first) Gulf War: between 142,000 and 206,000. *Source:* Ahtisaari report (UN, 1991); Daponte, 1993.

2. United Nations Children's Fund (UNICEF) estimated that half a million Iraqi children under the age of five died between 1991 and 1998. They would have lived if pre-sanctions trends of declining mortality had continued. Source: UNICEF, Child and Maternal Mortality Survey 1999, Preliminary Report, Baghdad, July 1999.

3. "Acute malnutrition among young children in Iraq has nearly doubled since the United States led an invasion of the country 20 months ago, according to surveys by the United Nations, aid agencies and the interim Iraqi government. After the rate of acute malnutrition among children younger than 5 steadily declined to 4 percent two years ago, it shot up to 7.7 percent this year, according to a study conducted by Iraq's Health Ministry in cooperation with Norway's Institute for Applied International Studies and the UN Development Program. The new figure translates to roughly 400,000 Iraqi children suffering from 'wasting,' a condition characterized by chronic diarrhea and dangerous deficiencies of protein." *Washington Post Foreign Service,* Sunday, November 21, 2004, Page A01.

APPENDIX

THE SYKES-PICOT AGREEMENT

1. Sir Edward Grey to Paul Cambon, 15 May 1916

I shall have the honour to reply fully in a further note to your Excellency's note of the 9th instant, relative to the creation of an Arab

State, but I should meanwhile be grateful if your Excellency could assure me that in those regions which, under the conditions recorded in that communication, become entirely French, or in which French interests are recognised as predominant, any existing British concessions, rights of navigation or development, and the rights and privileges of any British religious, scholastic, or medical institutions will be maintained.

His Majesty's Government are, of course, ready to give a reciprocal assurance in regard to the British area.

2. Sir Edward Grey to Paul Cambon, 16 May 1916

I have the honour to acknowledge the receipt of your Excellency's note of the 9th instant, stating that the French Government accept the limits of a future Arab State, or Confederation of States, and of those parts of Syria where French interests predominate, together with certain conditions attached thereto, such as they result from recent discussions in London and Petrograd on the subject.

I have the honour to inform your Excellency in reply that the acceptance of the whole project, as it now stands, will involve the abdication of considerable British interests, but, since His Majesty's Government recognise the advantage to the general cause of the Allies entailed in producing a more favourable internal political situation in Turkey, they are ready to accept the arrangement now arrived at, provided that the co-operation of the Arabs is secured, and that the Arabs fulfil the conditions and obtain the towns of Homs, Hama, Damascus, and Aleppo.

It is accordingly understood between the French and British Governments—

1. That France and Great Britain are prepared to recognize and protect an independent Arab State or a Confederation of Arab States in the areas (A) and (B) marked on the annexed map, under the suzerainty of an Arab chief. That in area (A) France, and in area (B) Great Britain, shall have priority of right of enterprise and local loans. That in area (A) France, and in area (B) Great Britain, shall alone supply advisers or foreign functionaries at the request of the Arab State or Confederation of Arab States.

2. That in the blue area France, and in the red area Great Britain, shall be allowed to establish such direct or indirect administration or control as they desire and as they may think fit to arrange with the Arab State or Confederation of Arab States.

3. That in the brown area there shall be established an international administration, the form of which is to be decided upon after consultation

with Russia, and subsequently in consultation with the other Allies, and the representatives of the Shereef of Mecca.

4. That Great Britain be accorded (1) the ports of Haifa and Acre, (2) guarantee of a given supply of water from the Tigris and Euphrates in area (A) for area (B). His Majesty's Government, on their part, undertake that they will at no time enter into negotiations for the cession of Cyprus to any third Power without the previous consent of the French Government.

5. That Alexandretta shall be a free port as regards the trade of the British Empire, and that there shall be no discrimination in port charges or facilities as regards British shipping and British goods; that there shall be freedom of transit for British goods through Alexandretta and by railway through the blue area, whether those goods are intended for or originate in the red area, or (B) area, or area (A); and there shall be no discrimination, direct or indirect against British goods on any railway or against British goods or ships at any port serving the areas mentioned.

That Haifa shall be a free port as regards the trade of France, her dominions and protectorates, and there shall be no discrimination in port charges or facilities as regards French shipping and French goods. There shall be freedom of transit for French goods through Haifa and by the British railway through the brown area, whether those goods are intended for or originate in the blue area, area (A), or area (B), and there shall be no discrimination, direct or indirect, against French goods on any railway, or against French goods or ships at any port serving the areas mentioned.

6. That in area (A) the Baghdad Railway shall not be extended southwards beyond Mosul, and in area (B) northwards beyond Samarra, until a railway connecting Baghdad with Aleppo via the Euphrates Valley has been completed, and then only with the concurrence of the two Governments.

7. That Great Britain has the right to build, administer, and be sole owner of a railway connecting Haifa with area (B), and shall have a perpetual right to transport troops along such a line at all times.

It is to be understood by both Governments that this railway is to facilitate the connexion of Baghdad with Haifa by rail, and it is further understood that, if the engineering difficulties and expense entailed by keeping this connecting line in the brown area only make the project unfeasible, that the French Government shall be prepared to consider that the line in question may also traverse the polygon Banias-Keis Marib-Salkhab Tell Otsda-Mesmie before reaching area (B).

8. For a period of twenty years the existing Turkish customs tariff shall remain in force throughout the whole of the blue and red areas, as

well as in areas (A) and (B), and no increase in the rates of duty or conversion from ad valorem to specific rates shall be made except by agreement between the two Powers.

There shall be no interior customs barriers between any of the above-mentioned areas. The customs duties leviable on goods destined for the interior shall be collected at the port of entry and handed over to the administration of the area of destination.

9. It shall be agreed that the French Government will at no time enter into any negotiations for the cession of their rights and will not cede such rights in the blue area to any third Power, except the Arab State or Confederation of Arab States without the previous agreement of His Majesty's Government, who, on their part, will give a similar undertaking to the French Government regarding the red area.

10. The British and French Governments, as the protectors of the Arab State, shall agree that they will not themselves acquire and will not consent to a third Power acquiring territorial possessions in the Arabian peninsula, nor consent to a third Power installing a naval base either on the east coast, or on the islands, of the Red Sea. This, however, shall not prevent such adjustment of the Aden frontier as may be necessary in consequence of recent Turkish aggression.

11. The negotiations with the Arabs as to the boundaries of the Arab State or Confederation of Arab States shall be continued through the same channel as heretofore on behalf of the two Powers.

12. It is agreed that measures to control the importation of arms into the Arab territories will be considered by the two Governments.

I have further the honour to state that, in order to make the agreement complete, His Majesty's Government are proposing to the Russian Government to exchange notes analogous to those exchanged by the latter and your Excellency's Government on the 26th April last. Copies of these notes will be communicated to your Excellency as soon as exchanged.

I would also venture to remind your Excellency that the conclusion of the present agreement raises, for practical consideration, the question of the claims of Italy to a share in any partition or rearrangement of Turkey in Asia, as formulated in article 9 of the agreement of the 26th April, 1915, between Italy and the Allies.

His Majesty's Government further consider that the Japanese Government should be informed of the arrangement now concluded.

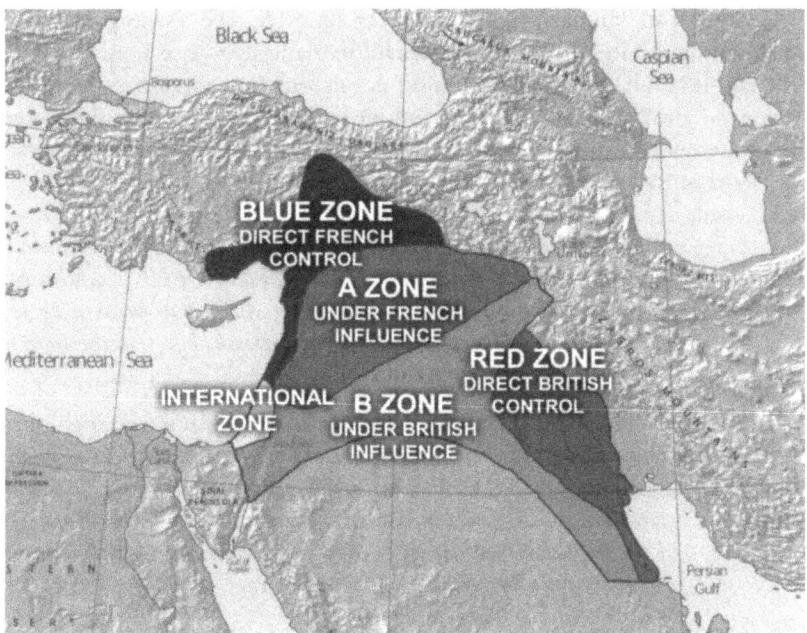

The Sykes-Plcot Agreement divided Iraq into the regions shown on this map.

QUOTES

"Making conservative assumptions, they estimated that around 100,000 Iraqi civilians died as a result of the invasion—mostly violent deaths among women and children related to military activity—and that the risk of death was about 25-fold higher after the invasion than before."

> —The Lancet, *October 29, 2004, citing the Center for International Emergency Disaster and Refugee Studies, Johns Hopkins Bloomberg School of Public Health, Baltimore, Maryland (L. Roberts, Ph.D., G Burnham, M.D.); Department of Community Medicine, College of Medicine, Al-Mustansiriya University, Baghdad, Iraq (R. Lafta, M.D., J Khudhairi, M.D.); and School of Nursing, Columbia University, New York (R. Garfield, Ph.D.)*

"We don't do body counts."

> —*General Tommy Franks, US Central Command*

"The very provisions of the Charter of the United Nations and the Declaration of Human Rights are being set aside. We are waging a war, through the United Nations, on the children and people of Iraq, and with incredible results: results that you do not expect to see in a war under the Geneva Conventions. We're targeting civilians. . . . I had been instructed to implement a policy that satisfies the definition of genocide: a deliberate policy that had effectively killed well over a million individuals, children and adults."

> —*Denis Halliday, upon his resignation in 1998 as Assistant Secretary-General of the United Nations and the UN Coordinator of Humanitarian Relief to Iraq. After thirty-four years with the United Nations, he resigned in protest over the effects of the embargo on the civilian population.*

"How long should the civilian population of Iraq be exposed to such punishment for something they have never done?"

> —*Hans Von Sponeck, who had succeeded Denis Halliday as Humanitarian Coordinator in Baghdad, resigned on February 13, 2000. Like Halliday, he had been with the United Nations for more than thirty years.*

Source: John Pilger, *The New Rulers of the World* (Verso, 2002)

Madeleine Albright, US ambassador to the United Nations, with
President Bill Clinton.

"I think this is a very hard choice, but the price—we think the price is
worth it."

—*Madeleine Albright, US ambassador to the United Nations,*
60 Minutes, *May 12, 1996*

US soldiers' coffins, Operation Enduring Freedom, Afghanistan

VI

"Blood and Oil":
The Human Costs of War

War does not determine who is right—only who is left.
—Bertrand Russell

GEORGE W. BUSH (State of the Union speech, January 29, 2003): And if war is forced upon us, we will fight with the full force and might of the United States military—and we will prevail.

DAVID CLINE: I was watching Bush in the State of the Union message. . . . It was a presentation to the American public, trying to hit buttons and stuff like that—not a very good one, I don't think. Well, when he was talking about war, he'd either get this solemn face or he'd get this stern face, but he was trying to get you to thinking, "Yeah, we're going to kick their ass. . . . Yeah, we're going to show them what's right." The reality is, they're going to kill a lot of people, you know. And that's what's all left out of that whole picture—they're going to kill a lot of people. Americans are going to die, Iraqis are going to die, large numbers of Iraqi civilians, who aren't holding guns at all, are going to die.

ARCHBISHOP DESMOND TUTU (speaking at the February 15, 2003, antiwar demonstration in New York City): Those who are going to be killed in Iraq are not collateral damage. They are human beings of flesh and blood. They are children, they are mothers, they are brothers, they are

117

grandfathers. You know what? They are our sisters and brothers. So, we belong in one family. We are members of one family, God's family, the human family.

ROGER NORMAND: I was part of a Center for Economic and Social Rights delegation to Iraq—a fact-finding mission in January of 2003. It had several purposes. One of them was a humanitarian assessment. And we came out with a report called "The Human Costs of War," . . . based on our visits to hospitals and clinics, based on our interviews with UN officials, government officials, and based on a whole set of confidential UN documents that we were able to get. The report makes very clear that there will be a humanitarian disaster in the event of war. And not only that, the United Nations, the independent relief agencies, and the Iraqi government are totally unprepared to deal with it. The problem that we see today is that the lessons of the first Gulf War have not been learned by the world, certainly not by the United States, not by the Pentagon. They're planning once again to target electricity; only this time the impact will be far, far worse. You'll have far more casualties because whereas in 1991 Iraq was a wealthy country, relatively speaking, today, after twelve years of sanctions, there's no middle class left. The vast majority of Iraqis are dependent for their survival on the Oil for Food program.

VICTOR SIDEL: Based on the weakened state of the Iraqi population, based on the weakened structure of hospitals and food supplies and food distribution in Iraq, the report by MEDACT suggested that a military attack at this time on Iraq would lead to vast civilian damage. The estimates of MEDACT range from 50,000 to over 200,000 civilian deaths as a result of a military attack. One of the imponderables, of course—one of the things that are impossible to predict—is what weapons will be used in an attack on Iraq. There is some danger that the United States may use earth-penetrating weapons that are based on nuclear weapons, in an attempt to destroy underground bunkers, an attempt to destroy what they feel may be underground stores of chemical and biological weapons. The danger of these earth-penetrating weapons is that, first of all, they are very unlikely to destroy underground stacks of chemical and biological weapons, if those exist. They will simply disperse them into the environment and not destroy them. And furthermore, and, in a way, even more dangerous, the use of nuclear weapons would open the door to further use of nuclear weapons, which [have] not been used in war, of course, since the United States used them in 1945 on Hiroshima and Nagasaki. Another weapon that has been discussed is a weapon that produces an electronic pulse of such a magnitude that it cuts off power supplies. That will, of course, affect power in hospitals, power to move food supplies, [and] will have a direct effect on the health of the civilian population.

NOAM CHOMSKY: In fact, it's kind of interesting the way this is now; just the last few days, there have been the first articles appearing saying that . . . Washington is beginning to take into account the risks of the war. There was one in the *New York Times* the other day. Take a look at the risks—the risks exclude totally the concerns of the aid agencies, the UN and so on, that there could be a horrible humanitarian catastrophe; now that's not even mentioned. The risks are the costs to the United States. So, they quote Rumsfeld, and you know he has a catalogue, a big thick book full of risks, and these are the risks that the US government and the *New York Times*, and the elites see—risks to us. Now, to be precise, there is a mention of risks to Iraqis. Namely, it said, "Saddam Hussein might use chemical weapons against Iraqis and blame it on us." That's the risk. We might be blamed for it. Or, things might go wrong and that would alienate the population. So, like if half a million people died, it might alienate the population and that will be bad for us—that's the only reason, it would be bad for us. The *Wall Street Journal* a couple of days later had an article on these very fancy . . . they were all excited in the military that they've got these wonderful new weapons that—it's kind of like my ten-year-old grandson playing a video game—they can use them against these . . . these creatures who can't shoot back and so on and so forth—it's going to be great fun. But they're worried about some of them, what they call e-weapons. Now the e-weapons will instantly and permanently wipe out the electrical power or other systems, which means massive biological warfare, exactly what it means. You wipe out power systems, water systems, sewage systems, and so on, what happens to the people in a city? OK, huge biological warfare and they say, "Well, we're kind of holding off on using these because it might harm US forces too and we haven't really perfected it yet and, again, it might kind of alienate the population. . . ." So that's why we might not use them—it's the only possible reason.

GEORGE W. BUSH (Cincinnati Museum Center speech, October 7, 2002): America is a friend to the people of Iraq.

JACQUELINE SOOHEN: I was in contact with the people of Iraq through most of the bombing until the very end when the telephone lines were all destroyed. One of the families I was really close to was [headed up by] Kareema. She's a single mother. She has eight kids—two sons and six daughters. They're the most beautiful daughters you've ever seen. The oldest one is 16. The one I was really close to, her name was Amalla. She was

13. She turned 14 the second day of the bombing. And I haven't heard from her since. And similarly, my friend Hyder. He's also a student. He's 20 and he was away, . . . out of the country in Jordan, for a school vacation and he could've stayed and avoided the war. And he decided to come back to be with his family. And he spent the last three weeks, every day . . . he'd call me every night, and often he'd call me in tears, because he kept trying to convince his mother to leave with his two younger sisters. And she wouldn't leave him alone. She wouldn't leave his father alone. And I don't know if they decided to leave. I don't know if they're still in Baghdad. I do know that the neighborhood that they live in was bombed very severely by the United States. And what's striking to me is that we never see these faces. We always see the faces of Iraqi officials. We always see the picture of Saddam Hussein. We never see the pictures of the Iraqi people.

EDMUND WHITE: I think that part of the problem in America is that people have a hard time picturing what these people look like. I mean, there are some great movies that have been made by the Iranians, especially Kiarostami, and it seems to me a shame that movies like those can't be seen by more Americans. Because I think—it sounds stupid—but I think that if people could picture individual people and see children and see women and see old men and see very nice people living ordinary lives and then imagine that they're all going to be destroyed, it would put a human face on this situation. The last Iraqi war, there was a lot of talk in America about how no civilians suffered. There was surgical bombing—they always use this [phrase] "surgical bombing." In fact, we now know that many civilians suffered terribly in that war. And certainly . . . the consequences, the economic consequences of that war have been terrible for the Iraqi people. But, most Americans don't realize it. They really imagine that the last war was won by a few well-placed bombs that killed nobody, that only destroyed armaments, or soldiers, but that civilians weren't touched. Well, this is a terrible myth and I think people imagine that this new war will be like that too. So, it reduces the problem of thinking we're going to murder lots of innocent people.

NORMAN SOLOMON: In December of 2002 I accompanied Sean Penn, the actor and director, to Baghdad. It was a trip organized by the Institute for Public Accuracy. It was difficult as an American to be a part of the hospital where children were dying and to realize that it was the US government really, not entirely but to a significant extent, responsible for their deaths. And people in the United States don't want to deal with that reality for the most part because of the news media. They haven't had to deal with that reality. I think of the great American writer James Baldwin, who wrote of the people in the United States. He put it this way. He said, "They have destroyed and are destroying and do not know it and do not want to know it." But Baldwin went on to say, "It's not permissible that the authors of devastation should also be innocent. It is their innocence that constitutes the crime." And a few decades later as we look at what's happened in Iraq, clearly that kind of false innocence of the people in the United States which has been made more easy by the US news media—that phony innocence is really part of the crimes against humanity that have been inflicted on Iraq by the US government. In my name with my tax dollars—that's the reality for Americans.

> *It is certain, in any case, that ignorance, allied with power, is the most ferocious enemy justice can have.*
>
> —James Baldwin

GORE VIDAL: President John Quincy Adams said in 1821, on the subject of our fighting to liberate Greece from Turkey, "the United States goes not abroad in search of monsters to destroy. If the United States took up all foreign affairs, she might become the dictatress of the world but she would no longer be the ruler of her own spirit or soul." Should we be allowed in 2004 to hold a presidential election here in the homeland? I suspect we shall realize that the only regime change that need concern our regained "spirit or soul" is in Washington. President Adams is long since dead. And we have now been in the empire business since at least 1900 with the conquest of the Philippines. The local population didn't want us there. We promised them independence. We killed 220,000 of them while subduing them. A few years ago there was a significant exchange between the then-General Colin Powell and the then-statesperson Madeleine Albright. Like so many civilians, she was eager to use our troops against one of our many, many, many enemies—every way we look there is somebody lurking who might want to find a special death threat and turn it on us. One can hardly sleep at night knowing [of] these dangers all around us. When Powell said no, she said: "What's the point of having all this military and not using it?" He said: "They are not toy soldiers." But in the interest of fighting communism we did spend trillions of dollars, until we are now threatening to sink under the weight of so much weaponry; much of it we have shifted over on Afghanistan and Iraq. So why not stop fooling around with diplomacy and treaties and coalitions and just use our military power to give orders to the rest of the world? Last summer Congress received from the administration a document called "The National Security Strategy of the United States." As the historian Joseph Stromberg observed, "It must be read to be believed." The doctrine preaches the desirability of the United States becoming, to use Adams's words, "dictatress of the world." It used to be Nicaragua was quite enough, you know. Now it is going to be Korea, China. . . . It also assumes that the president and his lieutenants are morally entitled to govern this planet. It declares that our "best defense is a good offense." The doctrine of preemption is next declared: "As a matter of common sense and self-defense, America will act against such emerging threats before they are fully formed." Now, this is a kind of madness. This is not what we started the country for. It's not what the rest of the world wants.

GEORGE W. BUSH (State of the Union speech, January 29, 2003): All free nations have a stake in preventing sudden and catastrophic attacks. And we're asking them to join us, and many are doing so. Yet the course of this nation does not depend on the decisions of others.

ROGER NORMAND: We're witnessing a unique event in the history of the United Nations—an event that possibly signals the end of the United Nations as we know it. The UN was established after World War II, when the world came together with a moral consensus that this could never happen again. What that meant is [prevention of] an unrestrained war—a war in which civilians were targeted without common legal principles that would restrain all parties, both sides, from ever doing that again. The fundamental purpose in Article 1 of the United Nations charter is to avert the scourge of war that twice in our lifetime has bought untold sorrow to mankind. That basic principle and that basic purpose of the United Nations has been fundamentally challenged now by the United States and Britain because they've circumvented the Security Council. They needed another resolution for this to be a legal war and they failed to get it. But rather than abiding by the rules, President Bush has said very plainly, "The words don't count. They don't matter anymore. We're going to war anyway." Not only that, it's . . . what he calls "a preventive war." It's really not a war, it's an invasion by the most powerful country in the world of a relatively small, weak country, whose entire economy—and, of course, the military as well—has been subject to twelve years of sanctions. But I think the most important thing here is that if we throw out the UN charters as the United States is doing, what are we left with? What we're left with is the situation before World War II. And that was where Germany, for example, launched invasions—what they called "preemptive war" against, say, Norway and Denmark. That was judged by the world at the Nuremberg Tribunals. And it was judged to be, in the words of the tribunal, "the supreme international crime." So, we're going back to a period where it's now legitimate for the most powerful countries in the world to commit what used to be understood as the supreme international crime. And so, because the United Nations or because the Security Council failed the world—failed in upholding the UN charters' fundamental purpose, failed because the United States wouldn't allow it to do its job—it falls to the rest of us. It falls to the civil society. It falls to the general public who have spoken very strongly against this war, to try to enforce international law through the International Criminal Court, through the concept of universal jurisdiction for war crimes.

REED BRODY: The new International Criminal Court, which was over-whelmingly voted by 120 to 7 in 1998 in Rome, . . . is probably going to be the most important human rights institution created in the last fifty years. This is the court that is going to be able to investigate and to prose-cute the Saddam Husseins, the Auguste Pinochets, the Pol Pots, the Idi Amins of the future. It is not a panacea. It is not going to stop the crimes from happening; but hopefully, over time, the existence of an internation-al justice system to punish the perpetrators of the worst atrocities is going to change the way countries are governed and international relations are organized. I think it is one of the things, frankly, that the US fears. The policy makers and the Bush administration and the Pentagon believe that the United States is the most powerful country in the world and it is not in their national interest to subject American use of power, American war making, to the constraints of the rule of law.

JOSE ALVAREZ: I think the fear goes way back in American history—that is, this notion that the US could be subject to court jurisdiction outside the four corners of the US. [It] goes back to this notion that nobody can second-guess the US and that our institutions for justice are the best in the world—and this notion of US exceptionalism pervades. It is particularly difficult for other countries to accept, because the US is the first to suggest that they should be subject to the international criminal process. We were strong advocates of the international tribunal for Rwanda, for the former Yugoslavia; we supported it financially, and that's a clear case of . . . "inter-national justice is good for you but not for us."

CURT GOERING: The United States was one of the handful of countries that didn't ratify this treaty. And, although President Clinton signed the treaty [on] his last day in office before he left, the new administration, the Bush administration coming in, unsigned the treaty. It was almost unheard of—that type of action where a successor government unsigns a treaty that a previous government has signed. And, not only did it unsign but it was so hostile and it is so hostile to that treaty, or indeed almost, it seems, [hostile to] any form of international standard, whether it's a human rights standard, whether it's an environmental standard or whatever, that seems to interfere with its way of doing business.

JOSE ALVAREZ: The administration has been quite clear that it opposes the International Criminal Court. And it opposes it precisely for the reason that it could put a US serviceperson, or those higher up, on trial. In fact the US made quite clear its position during the negotiations for the International Criminal Court at Rome. And since there has been legislation passed in Congress that suggests that we would be able to do certain nasty things to certain governments if they ratified the International Criminal Court, . . . it is clear that the opposition extends not just [to] the administration but also [to] majorities in both houses of Congress.

CURT GOERING: And now, at [this] moment, we see the United States actively using its military muscle, its economic muscle, to threaten other governments that have signed the treaty not to cooperate with the treaty. And to sign special agreements with the United States, which specify that those countries will not turn over any American soldier or civilian to the International Criminal Court. And there is immense pressure now on small countries like East Timor or Bulgaria or Romania to sign these bilateral treaties with the United States indicating that they won't, in effect, respect the provisions of the International Criminal Court when it comes to United States soldiers. It's an absolute catastrophe.

GEORGE W. BUSH (speech given at the United Nations General Assembly, September 12, 2002) : The United Nations was born in the hope that survived the World War, the hope of a world moving toward justice escaping all patterns of conflict and fear. The founding members resolved that the peace of the world must never again be destroyed by the will and weakness of any man. We created a United Nations Security Council. . . .

SCOTT RITTER: The United States is a member of the Security Council—in fact, one of five permanent members with the veto capability. The United Sates voted for a resolution calling for Iraq's disarmament, but since 1991, the United States has maintained a policy of regime removal which has taken priority over the international mandate of disarmament. In 1998, the United States used the weapons inspections process as a vehicle of deliberately provoking a confrontation with the government of Iraq, and then the United States ordered the weapons inspectors out. They weren't kicked out by Saddam Hussein, they were ordered out by the United States; and then the United States began a unilateral military campaign,

Operation Desert Fox, in which eighty-six of ninety-seven targets that were bombed by the United States . . . had nothing to do with disarmament and everything to do with the security of Saddam Hussein. Remember, the United States' policy of regime removal . . . sought to eliminate Saddam Hussein through military action—military action that was empowered by intelligence information gathered through the inspections process. The United States corrupted the inspections process by using it for purposes other than that mandated by the Security Council.

I spent seven years as an inspector in Iraq. It's frustrating work. We didn't get the full cooperation of the Iraqi government, but we have to keep this in mind: During those seven years, you know, every inspector came home alive and no American soldiers had to die and we didn't kill any Iraqi civilians. We accomplished quite a bit in the field of disarmament. We were able to ascertain a 90–95 percent level of accounting for these weapons as well as a 100 percent accounting for the factories used by Iraq to produce these weapons. . . . We don't know what the final disposition is of some critical aspects of the Iraqi programs, but there is no evidence that Iraq retains weapons of mass destruction today. When we talk about the inspection process today. . . . Remember the inspectors today are getting much better access than we ever enjoyed when I was an inspector, and it appears as though they're being successful. They haven't found any weapons of mass destruction. And as long as the inspectors are in Iraq, getting the full access they need, there's no way Iraq can rebuild these weapons of mass destruction. So, of course, the weapons inspection process must be respected. It is, after all, not only the rule of law, but it is a method of dealing with a critical situation that doesn't involve going to war, doesn't involve the loss of life. We must give the inspections a chance. We have no choice but to give the inspections a chance if we want to call ourselves a law-abiding people.

ROGER NORMAND: President Bush was never interested in disarmament. That disarmament never had a chance. . . . Even though the leader of disarmament, Hans Blix, asked for more time. Even though the Security Council made very reasonable proposals. "Just give them more time. Let them see what they can find. Help them. Support them." President Bush said: "No. We want war. It's about the removal of Saddam Hussein."

GEORGE W. BUSH (addressing the nation, March 17, 2003): Saddam Hussein and his sons must leave Iraq within forty-eight hours. The refusal to do so would resolve in military conflict commenced at a time of our choosing. For their own safety all foreign nationals, including journalists and inspectors, should leave Iraq immediately.

The victor will never be asked if he told the truth.

—Adolf Hitler

GORE VIDAL: When you live with nothing but lies being told you in the media, nothing but lies; and it's done the way they do advertising—it's repetition. "Weapons of mass destruction, he's got weapons of mass destruction, mass destruction, mass destruction." When you hear that ten thousand times a day you finally think he must have [them], you know. . . . Well, he didn't have them. Now, I'm sure we're busy planting them, you know, all over the place. And we will discover [them]: "Oh, look what we found. Goodness me, here's an atom bomb. Made in the USA. No, no, no. Scratch that out. Scratch that out." . . . I fully expect us to plant something or other. But as it's United State of Amnesia, why go through the trouble? It's expensive to have troops going around looking for stuff. I think, they think the public would've forgotten it. I think the public is forgetting it; it doesn't much care. I thought when I said that we would lose the war, I still think we will. Afghanistan—the fighting is going on rather rougher than it was during the so-called war. It'll keep right on going as long as we have a presence in Iraq, and we'll eventually be driven out. Somebody will have a bright idea—one of those neo-conservatives, and we know what they're like. They'll decide to kill everybody there, that this would be a very good thing to do—"gotta show force." And all these sissies, you know, all of whom ran from the idea of going into the Army talk so tough when they get together: "Boy, we're gonna show our muscle." You know, fat boys with asthma talking tough. It makes the blood run cold.

GEORGE W. BUSH (State of the Union speech, January 29, 2003): The war goes on, and we are winning.

GORE VIDAL: So, I think that we haven't a chance of winning in the Middle East; nobody else has. Nobody except the Turks with the Ottoman Empire, which Woodrow Wilson, one of the great fools in our history, decided to break up after the end of World War I. So, we get Turkey, which turns out to be really quite a formed little country now. And broke up bits and pieces into Syria and into Jordan, into this into that, which formerly had been . . . then became French and British mandates and are now countries that are uneasy, with all sorts of warring religious groups.

Oil is much too important a commodity to be left in the hands of the Arabs.

—Henry Kissinger

VICTORIA DE GRAZIA: It's very, very important to see the long run—to see the Muslim areas adjacent to Europe as areas of conquests, re-conquests, or division, re-division. . . . The United States join[ed], in terms of project, the other colonial powers [France and Great Britain] in the course of the late 1930s. We have lots of evidence of that. And then, in the course of World War II, when the great old powers collapsed and were no longer able to control that area, the United States very quickly moved in, recognizing as the others did that this was now an area of petroleum and that petroleum was absolutely critical to the new phase of development.

GEORGE W. BUSH (addressing the nation, March 19, 2003): We have no ambition in Iraq except to remove a threat and restore control of that country to its own people.

HOWARD ZINN: Well, you know, it's very clear that the reasons given by the Bush administration for going into Iraq are empty. They fall apart immediately, you know; they don't make any sense—weapons of mass destruction. . . . You know, obviously, that's not what the Bush administration cares about because there are other countries with much greater weapons of mass destruction. [We] have eight nuclear powers. Iraq might have possibly one nuclear weapon in two years or three. . . . So, weapons of mass destruction is just really . . . it's just an argument made by the Bush administration to justify . . . you know. . . . I believe, you know, the chief reason for the United States' fussing with Iraq is a question of oil. The administration, of course, doesn't want to talk about oil. It would rather not talk about oil, because as soon as you talk about oil, it brings up all those banners that people carry saying, "No blood for oil." . . . But . . . [at] the end of WWII, 1945, President Roosevelt met with Ibn Saud of Saudi Arabia and they made an agreement and the agreement was that the United States would now become the major player in the oil fields in the Middle East, and in return, the United States would maintain the Saudi monarchy in power. Now, ever since then, oil has been at the center of American Middle East policy. I mean, it was the reason for the United States' overthrow of the Mossadegh regime in Iran in 1953. The reason for everything the United States has done. The reason for the first Gulf War. Sure, the argument, the excuse was Kuwait, invasion of Kuwait. But who can believe that the Bush administration was really heartbroken over the invasion of Kuwait? After all, the Bush administration has seen many invasions of many countries . . . —including by the United States—and, no problem, you see. . . . So, oil was behind it, no question—and today, no doubt about it. You know, Iraq has the second-largest oil reserves in the Middle East and the United States is determined to get control of them and Saddam Hussein stands in the way.

NOAM CHOMSKY: Well, one long-term objective of the United States— you'd have to be a political idiot not to know it—is to extend and intensify its control over the world's major energy resources, and there's a simple way to do that—or, it's not so simple—but an obvious way to do it and that is to regain control over Iraq's resources, which are the second largest in the world and to be able to establish major military bases for the first time right at the heart of the oil-producing region. The United States . . . does not intend to use the oil—it's never been an issue, even a secondary issue, [as it] has many more stable resources—but it does want to control it and that's been true since 1945 since it pushed out Britain and France from positions of world domination.

TIMOTHY MITCHELL: The United States doesn't have any problem having access to oil. It buys some of its oil from the Middle East, as do other countries, and it can also buy lots more. The oil question is the following: It is about profits from oil, and profits from oil depend on the control of the price, and the significance of Middle Eastern oil is that whoever controls Middle Eastern oil controls the price of oil. And because maintaining the price at the level that the US wants it at is done by restricting supply, I think it is more important to see that the United States is worried not about a scarcity of oil but, rather, about an overabundance of oil.

ROGER NORMAND: It's no coincidence, let's put it this way, that Iraq is part of the region that has the largest oil reserves in the world. Afghanistan is part of the region that has the second-largest oil reserves and the largest gas reserves in the world. And if you look at a map of the world right now and you see where the United States has established its military bases, you see just a ring all over Central Asia, all over the Middle East; all . . . the Middle Eastern countries, except five, now have a US military presence. Now, twelve years ago, this was inconceivable. It could not have been imagined that US troops would be based throughout the Persian Gulf in Saudi Arabia—the home of Mecca, the heart of Islam. This could not have been imagined, yet now there's hardly a country that doesn't have a US military base.

GREG PALAST: Condoleezza Rice was on the board of Chevron Oil. And, . . . there's a tanker, an oil tanker called the *Condoleezza*, named after her. And so, you can just see that, you know, when they say, "Is there an influence of oil in the Bush administration?" No, the oil companies *are* the Bush administration. So, you want to know [who] are gonna be the winners in this conflict. You have to look at who won the first conflict. After

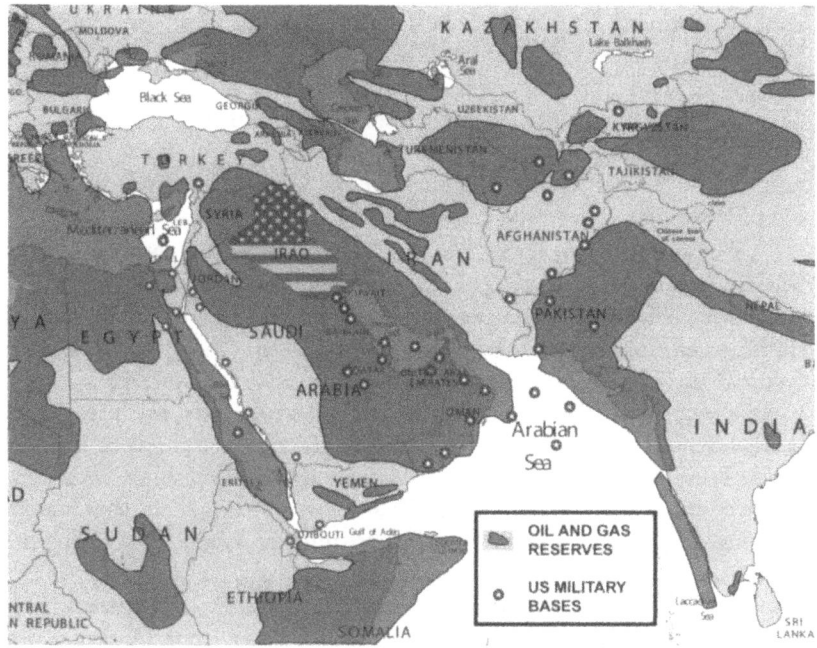

Oil and gas reserves and US military bases

the war we never got democracy in Kuwait as we were promised. Women, who had been driving around, had freedoms, suddenly were back under the veil. So, who won? The answer: Chevron Oil. Chevron got George Bush, the daddy, to write a letter to the Emirate of Kuwait asking for an oil concession for Chevron. Now, the Emirate can't say no because, after all, George Bush is the guy that saved all the Rolls Royces, right? So, he saved them so they could give the concession to Chevron Oil. And then Chevron Oil, by the way, turns around and gives half a million dollars and more to the Republican Party campaign for president—for Bush's son. Now, Bush himself got no money, but his son was well compensated, and needless to say his son was well compensated by Chevron. You know, obviously it didn't hurt that Bush had written a letter for them.

THE SECOND FRONT

GREG PALAST: Back to Hugo Chavez. So, you have tremendous disinformation coming out from the US press about Hugo Chavez, straight out of the

State Department. "He's a would-be dictator," says the *New York Times*. The guy won the majority of the vote. They didn't call George Bush a "would-be dictator" even though he lost the vote in America. Well, what is Hugo Chavez's real crime? One, he has a reform program which involves . . . which requires doubling the royalties on US oil companies, from 16 percent to about 30 percent for the oil pulled out of Venezuela—crude oil pulled out of Venezuela. Obviously, Condoleezza Rice doesn't really like that.

The second thing is that Hugo Chavez restored the power of OPEC because he was really running OPEC through the offices of the secondary general of OPEC, who is his personal ally—Ali Rodriguez. People think of OPEC as an Arab organization. In fact, it was Hugo Chavez who had control, and the US did not like that at all. Especially, the problem is that if [there's] war in the Middle East, you end up with losing oil fields there, [and] where do we get the oil? We'd have to get it from Venezuela. The last Arab oil embargo was smashed by ramping up production in Venezuela. We need control of that oil. Hugo Chavez has got to go. So, they started working on him through the Bush fingers into the media, controlling the media [saying] that Hugo Chavez is crazy, he's a nut, and therefore we can support and help a *coup d'état* against him. That is what I call a second hidden front in the oil wars; [it] is our attack, our quiet undermining of the Venezuelan government.

WEAPONS OF MASS DESTRUCTION/DISTRACTION

GREG PALAST: Iraq has become the weapon of mass distraction. Everyone's looking at Iraq. Even the left is looking at Iraq and forgetting everything else that's going on. Not only Venezuela, which we're all ignoring. But one of the things I've been working on is what the World Trade Organization, the IMF, and the World Bank, which are kind of the financial arms, the financial enforcement agencies of the new world order, [the] economic order—what they're up to. I have obtained thousands, literally thousands of pages of documentation inside of those organizations. Let me show you some. . . . All marked secret, all marked confidential—about what they're really doing to tear apart Argentina, Ecuador, etc. In fact, I'm now trying to work . . . I'm working with Noam Chomsky on analyzing the secret papers I have from the World Bank about what they intend to do to Turkey. . . . If they help out the US in war, they'll be given a pass, but not much. Part of the program is that the IMF has forced the nation to raise its interest rates, causing their budget to fall short by $9 billion. The US government is going to give them $8 billion. So, basically the US government is going to give them just enough to pay back the European and American banks, but not enough to survive. But if they don't get that money, they will be hung out to dry and all their assets—power companies, water companies, bridges, ports, you name it—are going to be sold off to the European and American consortium.

THE MISSING LINK

ARNO MAYER: As far as this crisis around Iraq is concerned, my point of departure in reflecting on it is a rather bizarre one in that, it seems to me, that even if I list all the causes that people have given for America's—oh, the Bush administration's—fixation on Iraq and Saddam Hussein, namely the problem with the father, namely oil, the political reasons, and so on and so forth, it seems to me that there is still a missing link because quite frankly, I don't get it as to why and how the Bush administration came to cathect onto Iraq and Saddam Hussein the way they have during the past year and a half. Though it must be admitted that, in terms of some of the advisors around him, they were, of course, not obsessed but nevertheless very much preoccupied with the Iraq problem even before Bush came to the White House. In any case, it seems to me that the big question is as to why in America it's extremely difficult to raise fundamental questions about what the project, the larger project, of this fixation on Iraq might really involve. I don't think that there is anything dishonorable, about, for example, bringing into the discussion the problem of oil. One does not have to be either a Marxist, or if not a Marxist, a materialist, or if not a materialist, one doesn't have to be an enemy of America in order to say that there may be an oil interest that is at work because, after all, oil has been at the center of the politics and the diplomacy of the great powers since before WWI.

I need not go now into the way in which Iraq, shall we say, was constructed immediately after WWI. But it was constructed as part of a negotiation for the reorganization of the legacy of the Ottoman Empire between Britain and France. One can be indignant about it, but it's a fact of life. And likewise after WWII; once again the question came up as to just exactly how oil figures [into] the reconstruction that went on after 1945 and, it would seem to me, [it's] not altogether accidental that, after all, at the time of Mossadegh, Iran, again the oil factor played very heavily and that was in the early 1950s. When America took over, so to speak, the eastern Mediterranean from the British—Turkey and Greece and so on—that, too, was related to sort of taking over the imperial watch that

Britain had exercised for a whole century before the Americans got into this act. Anyway, that's certainly one aspect of it. For the Bush administration to maintain that Iraq, and in particular Saddam Hussein, is a threat to the world, including to the United States, really boggles the mind. In a piece that I wrote on this Iraq business, I tried to suggest that compared to the Soviet Union, which the United States with its allies successfully contained until 1989 without going to war, Iraq is a pygmy. So that, then, raises the question as to why the insistence on the direct military intervention, and quite frankly the answer to that I would not even know how to begin to address. I mean to formulate an answer, and that comes to the missing link.

APPENDIX

Number of states that have signed a Bilateral Immunity Agreement with the United States: 45 (as of June 2003)

Number of states that have been approached but have not signed a Bilateral Immunity Agreement with the United States: over 100 (as of June 2003)

Table VI.1. Number of Years, as of 2002, Selected Countries' Oil Reserves Are Expected to Last

Country	Years
United Kingdom	5.94
Canada	6.20
USA	10.52
Russian Federation	19.25
Venezuela	63.58
Azerbaijan	67.02
Iran	67.25
Saudi Arabia	85.13
United Arab Emirates	114.81
Kuwait	127.70
Iraq	128.98

Source: BP

George W. Bush, who has never served in a war, in uniform

"Pax Americana": US Hegemony

You may deceive all the people part of the time, and part of the people all the time, but not all of the people all the time.
—Abraham Lincoln, 16th US president (1861–1865)

GEORGE W. BUSH (Cincinnati Museum Center speech, October 7, 2002): International human rights groups have catalogued other methods used in the torture chambers of Iraq: electric shock, burning with hot irons, dripping acid on the skin, mutilation with electric drills, cutting out tongues, and rape. If this is not evil, then evil has no meaning.

CURT GOERING: To invoke human rights as a reason for military action to be taken when nothing else has been said or done previously, and with respect to Iraq where in fact throughout the 1980s the United States was giving a whole lot of political and economic support to the very Iraqi government which it has now dislodged. And with Secretary Rumsfeld going to Baghdad in order to shake hands with Saddam Hussein and convey the support of the US for the Iraqis in their fight against Iran. And with the increase in US agricultural credits that were being provided to Iraq throughout the 1980s and, in fact, which actually doubled after the Iraqis used chemical weapons against the Kurds in the north of the country in 1988. . . .

GEORGE W. BUSH (Cincinnati Museum Center speech, October 7, 2002): Saddam Hussein also has experience in using chemical weapons. He's ordered chemical attacks on Iran and on more than forty villages in his own country.

REED BRODY: I remember in 1989, after Saddam Hussein had laid waste to Kurdish villages using chemical weapons, I was working in Geneva advocating at the UN and we were trying to get the UN Human Rights Commission to criticize Iraqi policy and the United States refused to even co-sponsor a resolution put forward by fifteen European countries to criticize Saddam Hussein and his use of chemical weapons.

CURT GOERING: If human rights really were the reason that this administration was motivated, then it raises fundamental questions about Saudi Arabia, which is on very good terms with the US in many respects, [and about] Uzbekistan or Pakistan, where we have in effect now a military dictator who's with the US on that war on terror. The Russians in Chechnya have been committing massive human rights violations and yet, especially since this so-called war on terror started there, . . . it's been met with silence by the administration for the most part. And the US did not do much to promote the resolution at the recent Human Rights Commission in Geneva condemning Russia for the abuses in Chechnya. So, it's a very selective approach that the administration is taking on human rights. And in fact, I believe this administration . . . the United States . . . has lost now in the human rights debate globally because of its hypocrisy, because of its double standards, because it uses the term "human rights" when it's politically convenient or politically expedient. And it ignores it when it's too close to home.

REED BRODY: The hallmark of any human rights advocacy has to be consistency. It has to be talking about violations wherever they occurred and wherever they have been committed by your friend or by your foe. But you can't go soft on one day and then, to suit your purposes, demonize the same policy the next day. The political utilization of human rights threatens to undermine the entire ideal.

GEORGE W. BUSH (State of the Union speech, January 29, 2003): And as we and our coalition partners are doing in Afghanistan, we will bring to the Iraqi people food and medicines and supplies—and freedom.

GREG PALAST: We have a great democracy that we brought to Afghanistan. It's kind of a democracy. . . . The only people who get to vote, it seems, are warlords and drug lords. They get all the votes because they got all the guns, and that's it. You know, so democracy is not a major issue with the

Bush administration. Look, if they don't want democracy in Florida, they're not going to bother about democracy in Afghanistan.

VICTORIA DE GRAZIA: Well, it seems highly contradictory and implausible policy to make war to create a military dictatorship and to try to bring stability, much less democracy, to a large state, which Iraq is, in an enormously complicated area. If one looks back in American history to see when policies of empire building were successful—well, one sees a number of factors. The conditions in Italy and Germany and Japan were very, very different. First of all, the United States was very convinced by what it meant by "democracy." And this meant reforms of the economic structures such as to raise the standard of living combined with the vote—universal suffrage, which would be organized through centrist-type parties. But that was a very peculiar historical moment. It's not clear now what the importation or the exportation of democracy means. It's so unclear what will go toward forming a democratic government. But there are certainly no signs that this is in the offing, not least of the reasons being that in the entire area the United States has traditionally supported nondemocratic regimes—distinctly nondemocratic regimes.

TIMOTHY MITCHELL: None of the US allies in the region is a particularly democratic regime. There are four other governments that are of particular importance to the US. One is Saudi Arabia, which allows no form of democracy, which allows very, very little in the way of political freedom at all, and the US has never supported any of the reform or the democratic efforts going on within Saudi Arabia. The second major ally is Egypt, and there is a similar story. The United States policy toward Egypt is supporting the existing government in doing everything it can to help the government of Mubarak to stay in power. No concrete support is given to those Egyptians who have been fighting for a long time for increased political rights. Two other main allies are Israel and Turkey. There the situation is somehow different because both of those countries have a democratic form of government. Turkey is a country that has successfully maintained a form of democracy; it is one that has been interrupted repeatedly by military coups. And when the military has been actually seizing power, [it] has been playing a role in politics in governing who is allowed to even compete in politics and who is not. And it is also a country that in the course of the 1990s, in particular, was carrying out a very extensive political and military campaign against the Kurdish population in the east of the country, which was extraordinary violent. In Israel the democratic form of government is for Israeli Jews; and at the same time Israel occupies Palestinian territories and exercises over those a military dictatorship, so it is a rather limited form of democracy.

HANNY MEGALLY: Now, there is growing concern that a conflict in Iraq may spread to the rest of the region. There are fears that Jordan may become very unstable—and there is a large Palestinian population in Jordan. There has been talk in Israel of transfer of Palestinians to Jordan. And so people are concerned that Israel may use the cover of the war in

Israel and the Palestinian occupied territories

Iraq to also impose certain conditions in Israel, affecting the Palestinian population there and in the occupied territories.

TIMOTHY MITCHELL: The relationship between the Israeli-Palestinian conflict and the Iraq crisis is a complicated one. Of course the Israeli-Palestinian conflict has its own history, its own dynamic, [tracing] back to the events of 1948, and then more recently 1967, when the West Bank and Gaza came under Israeli occupation. And the current conflict, although it does relate back to those earlier events, is most specifically about the attempt by the Palestinians to end the occupation that was established in 1967. And the most recent phase of it is the uprising of Intifada that broke out in September of 2000. As the Intifada developed and the level of violence increased, there was one last effort [made] under the framework of the Oslo Process in 1993—an agreement between the Palestinians and the Israeli government. And that was a series of talks initiated by Bill Clinton, as earlier talks had been, but then continued by the Israelis and Palestinians, without actually any American role, in Taba—[the] Egyptian town of Taba—in January of 2001.

For the first time the Israeli government made a proposal for the boundaries of a Palestinian state in the occupied territories, [one] that offered the Palestinians a contiguous state. In the midst of that, two things happened. One was that Barak himself—he was already a kind of caretaker, prime minister—he had effectively resigned and was awaiting elections in February of 2001 and in fact was defeated in those elections and was replaced by Sharon. I think more importantly, Clinton—he also was a lame-duck president at that point, and was in the very midst of those talks—left office and the Bush government was inaugurated. The Bush administration made it quite clear that it was not interested in pursuing further the Clinton policy and refused to give any energy to . . . that process. Sharon came to power and announced that his solution for dealing with the Intifada was a military one. He was going to crush it, and he proceeded to attempt to crush it militarily in the spring of 2001.

HANNY MEGALLY: We have been monitoring, particularly over the last two years, the clashes between Israelis and Palestinians. Obviously there is an occupation which has been going on for fifty years, and Palestinians are resisting the occupation and have been resorting to the use of force. As a human rights organization we don't take positions on occupation or occupations *per se*, but actually [on] the conducts. Just as we don't take positions on wars but we try to monitor the conduct of all sides during a war. And in this case what we have been looking at are civilians on both sides and the impact of the clashes and the conflict on civilians. From the Israeli side we have been monitoring excessive use of force, excessive use of lethal force, arrests. We have been monitoring house demolitions. We have been monitoring the assassination policy by the Israeli defense forces. We are now concerned about policies that may include deportations or transfers of populations. There has been a host of violations that we have been looking at. Jenin is one example of when Israeli troops went in and where the team we sent in to look at what happened there found that war crimes may have been committed by the Israeli defense forces. We have also been looking at actions by the Palestinian armed groups. And in particular, as the world has come to see, the suicide bombings, which deliberately target civilians, have been happening more and more, are carried out more by armed groups and not by the Palestinian authority itself. And [they] constitute, in our opinion, crimes against humanity. We've looked, also, at the human rights record of the Palestinian authority and have been concerned about state security courts, allegations of torture, deaths in custody, etc.

CURT GOERING: The Israelis have been conducting massive human rights violations in so many areas over the past two and a half years and have essentially been given a green light by the Bush administration. Palestinians as well have been involved in, of course, suicide bombings and armed attacks against civilians, which are also crimes against humanity, and there's not enough being done to stop that. But the administration is virtually silent when abuses are committed by its friends.

TIMOTHY MITCHELL: The United States sent a mediator senator, George Mitchell—former senator George Mitchell—to the occupied territories to investigate. And Mitchell published a report and that report called for a cease-fire, but it also called for something else—specifically, for Israel to halt the building of the expansion of its settlements in the occupied territories. And the United States demanded that Israel accept that Mitchell report, specifically that element. And the Sharon government refused. Now, it's quite within the power of the United States government to actually enforce a halt to the building of settlements because those are possible only because of US financial and military aid.

UDI ALONI: What America [is doing] to Israel is really destroying Israel itself. . . . I speak as an Israeli and a Jew. . . . If Jewish people and Israeli people really love Israel, really want to see Israel live in peace, they really have to say no to George W. Bush. . . . If tomorrow it's worth his interest to support the Arabs and attack the Jews, he would do it. For him, the Jews and the Arabs are just toys to play his game.

AMIT MASHIAH (speaking at the February 15, 2003, anti-war demonstration in New York City): My name is Amit Mashiah. I come from Israel. I represent a group of 520 officers and soldiers of the Israeli army who refuse to serve in the occupied territories any longer.

ROGER NORMAND: What's interesting about Israel is that essentially what Israel has done in terms of foreign policy, in terms of military policy, in terms of its legal policy, is almost an advanced notice of what the United States will do. In many ways, Israel is field-testing American policies. What we're now going to see, I predict, is [a] US direct military occupation of Iraq in which there won't even be a pretense of Iraqi leadership. There will be an American military governor in place. We won't apply the Geneva Conventions, just as we don't apply the Geneva Conventions to the prisoners of war in Guantanamo. And we will have the Israeli example to cite. And it's not just that. There are direct military tactics—for example, what [are] called "targeted assassinations," which are clearly illegal because you're allowing your military to act as judge and jury of people [about whom] you don't yet know what they've done and what they haven't done, and innocent people are always killed. But Israel has been doing that for a long time in the territories—assassinations. Initially the US condemned these. Then they were quiet. Now we've done it ourselves in Yemen and I'm sure . . . it's now official policy. Bush had talks about that. Another example is Jenin. What Israel did in Jenin was condemned by every human rights group—Amnesty, Human Rights Watch, Israeli groups as well, Palestinian groups—as a war crime. What the United States did in response is set up a joint military exercise to learn the lessons of Jenin for urban combat that was expected to happen in Baghdad.

I think that right now, unfortunately, there is an incredible coincidence of strategy and interest between [the Bush administration and] the most extremist Israeli government there has ever been; that's the Sharon government. In his own government, Sharon is not the hard-liner. It's called the "transfer government" because you have major ministers, including the housing minister, who openly advocate the ethnic cleansing of Palestinians from their own homeland. This is not hidden. It's known in Israel as the "transfer government." Their counterpart in the United States, the Bush administration, is also the most extreme and radical . . . American government I think that we've ever seen—[one] in which the people who hold the key positions of policy, in our military and in our internal security, are not within the mainstream of the Republican Party. They're radical extremists. They are essentially fundamentalists, and here I would want to make the last link between the United States and Israel

. . . and this is quite well documented. There are very, very strong links [among] the Christian fundamentalist movements and the Israeli government, what I would call the Zionist Fundamentalist movement now represented by Sharon, and the US government [as well], in terms of millions of dollars of funding, in terms of political ties. So, what you have is a very dangerous combination—a religious or ideological fundamentalism allied to state power.

TIMOTHY MITCHELL: The policy currently being pursued by the Bush government of planning for a war against Iraq is a policy that is being promoted by particular individuals within the Bush administration with very close ties to Israel, not necessarily acting in Israel's behest in any way, but nevertheless, that sees . . . how the region might be reorganized and remade, in ways in which Israel is central, and the right and far right in Israel [are] very much in agreement. People like Richard Perle, people like Paul Wolfowitz, who are the most active proponents of a war against Iraq to overthrow Saddam Hussein, people who have a long history of close ties with Israel. Perle, in particular—when he was out of favor in Washington during the period of the Clinton administration, [he] worked closely with the far right in Israel [and] with Netanyahu in particular; [he] helped him formulate his own policies. And it was in that period that they actually formulated this much broader scheme for the Middle East in which the overthrow of the government of Iraq is one part. It is a scheme which seeks to abandon the increasingly unreliable US clients in Egypt and Saudi Arabia and make the United States much more directly reliant on Israel and perhaps on, and this is the way they envisage things, a US-occupied Iraq.

ROGER NORMAND: The people who are now in the White House and the Pentagon, in particular, and the State Department have written for more than ten years about the need to topple Saddam Hussein, to essentially take direct control of the oil fields in the Middle East and Afghanistan. I mean, this is public writing, this is publicly available. And the reason they want to do all of that is because they believe in a doctrine which has now been officially adopted by the Pentagon. It's called "Full-Spectrum Dominance." And what that means is, as they say, in a unipolar world, in a world where there's just one superpower, why should we, meaning the US government, be constrained from doing what we want, where we want, because we have the US military that can enable us to do that. It's about geopolitical control—establishing American power in the most important regions of the world. And, again, this is not a conspiracy theory; it's not even my opinion: It is what was written by people like Dick Cheney and

Sign at an anti-war demonstration, Washington, DC, October 26, 2002

Paul Wolfowitz and Richard Perle and Douglas Feith and all of the people who now hold not just important positions in the US government but the key positions in our military security complex right now.

NORMAN SOLOMON: Well, Bush is a true believer, but he's not the one who's put this administration together. It's been people like Cheney and Rumsfeld—and, yes, the "Project for a New American Century" was a really odious name, for starters. [See Appendix.] The notion that an entire century on the planet belongs to a particular country is rather megalomaniacal, you might say. So, 9/11 was a godsend for that agenda because it gave the United States the claim to be the victim in any future activity. I think that exploiting 9/11 was a process of the Bush administration moving forward, as though 9/11 is a license to kill.

OLD EUROPE

VICTORIA DE GRAZIA: It's hard to understand how the United States could create an open empire at a moment when the very openness of the world market created such a distress and undermining of political institutions. The only way that seems plausible is by some sort of multilateral efforts. So, even if one conceived of a Western colonialism, neo-colonialism, which has not been not spoken about to deal precisely with these problem areas, one would require a Western multilateral structure such as one could have through the UN or through some sort of joint operation with the Europeans—especially in [an] area like the Mediterranean, which is of enormous interest to the Europeans as they become more unified. And so, the United States policy to go at it alone seems so contradictory toward every form of good sense, even in an imperial framework.

TIMOTHY MITCHELL: The major threat to US power is not Saddam Hussein or any other potential regime in the region. It is much more Europe and the American concern [over] the rise of Europe, especially now the united Europe of the European Union as a rival global power and perhaps specifically the question of the European Union in alliance with Russia. And I think planners in Washington concerned about envisaging the remaking [of] political order in the Middle East have in mind much more the issue of competition with Europe, the fear of Europe in alliance with Russia becoming an economic power and a global power that would rival the United States.

ARNO MAYER: As far as America's relationship to Europe is concerned, it would seem to me that it's a perfectly natural reaction on Washington's part to raise some serious questions about how this newly constructed Europe will impact on the international system and, in particular, on the relationship . . . on the, shall we say, hegemony, that America, at the moment, exercises over large parts of the world. And there, I think, I would make one point in particular, and that is, if the rate of economic development in China that has been evident over the last few years, if that rate of economic development should continue for another fifteen or twenty years, that means that America is really worried about the time from now to then. There will be another countervailing power in the international system fifteen or twenty years down the road, and I'm thinking in particular of China. And then the question comes up as to what the relationship of the United States will be to Europe at a time when it will have to face up, down the road, to operating within an international system in which another major power begins to throw its weight around.

Now this recent sort of . . . disagreement between the Europeans and the Americans, and I shouldn't say "the Americans," "the Bush administration," . . . may well be related to the fact—I'm not saying that it is, but it may well be related to the fact—that the Europeans are quite aware of the fact that, militarily, they do not add up to very much. But in terms of the new Europe that has been constructed since 1945, Europe is beginning to add up to something economically, and one ought not to forget that that was the original intention when it all started with the Schuman Plan and so on. The original idea was, "We start with economics and then see, . . . once a certain economic base has been created, as to what"—I don't want to use Marxist language here but anyway—"what other political and social structures could be constructed . . . that would tie it more firmly together than economics alone would not be able to do." Now what is so interesting to me—at any rate, in this recent contretemps between Washington, on the one hand, and then Paris and Berlin, on the other—is that, after all, France and Germany, plus Benelux, represent the core of Europe; and when one says "the core of Europe," [one means] the core of this new European economy, which, by now, has a currency of its own, the Euro, which looks, at the moment, as if it were the only international currency that could, to some extent, measure itself with the dollar. There is no other one, as far as I know. And, it would seem to me, that that is again an issue that is not being explicitly addressed as one dances this diplomatic waltz around the issue of Iraq. Churchill during WWII very often spoke of the possibility of being able to get at the Germans by invading Europe's "soft underbelly"—and he was thinking of the Balkans, etc. Now we all know that the soft underbelly wasn't as soft as the phrase suggests. But at this time, it looks to me as if the Americans were trying to hit the soft underbelly of Europe—that is to say, the ex-satellites of the Soviet Union—and rally them around the position of Washington, . . . thereby complicating the further construction of the European Union and also the further construction of the European economy. Certainly, it seems to me, not that far-fetched to raise that as being one of the possible considerations at this moment when, on the one hand, Paris and Berlin and then, on the other, . . . Washington, are squaring off around the issue of Iraq. It is not Iraq that is the issue. I think Iraq represents an issue that reveals many things that have been going on under the surface and, at the same time, serves as an issue around which the major powers can redefine their positions.

DÉJÀ VU

> *The only way to attack a much weaker enemy is to construct a huge propaganda offensive depicting it as about to commit genocide, maybe even a threat to our very survival, then to celebrate a miraculous victory over the awesome foe, while chanting praises to the courageous leaders who came to the rescue just in time.*
>
> —Noam Chomsky

NOAM CHOMSKY: Well, that's actually a quote from an intelligence report
. . . to the first Bush administration in 1989. When a new administration
comes into office, it gets a review of the world situation from the intelligence agencies, and the Bush administration, of course, did—this is the
first Bush administration. And these are usually secret—in fact, always
secret. But parts of this one were leaked. It had to do with "confrontation
with a much weaker enemy"—that's their phrase. And it said, "In the case
of confrontation with a much weaker enemy, the United States must defeat
them decisively and rapidly," or else political support will erode because it's
very thin. It's not like the 1960s, when you can carry on a war for years and
nobody cares. Now it's very weak. You can only attack much weaker enemies, but then you have to gain . . . but you have to do it fast. But you
have to get some support for that too. And the only way you can do it is
. . . by, first of all, . . . magnifying them to awesome forces. So, just remember what these same people did through the 1980s, and Nicaragua was two
days' marching time from Texas, and so on and so forth—one ludicrous
claim after another. And then somehow, . . . you succeed in conquering
Grenada and save us from the Russian airbase or something like that.
Anyhow, that's what the interventions through the 90s have been—a con-
cocted enemy that is just about to commit genocide or maybe destroy us
and then [we] miraculously defeat them—even though they're an awesome
foe—and then march on to the next one. Now, this wasn't that important
for the Clinton administration, but it's extremely important for this [cur-
rent] administration because . . . these are the same people who ran the
country in the 80s, remember, so you want to figure out what they're
doing; just look at their record—the same people. They're carrying out
programs which are quite harmful to the general population. I mean, you
know, tax cut for the rich, and the whole rest of it, is harming people; people don't like it. So the public, as in the 80s—the public is strongly
opposed to almost all their policies.

Well, how do you keep people under control and continue to institute those policies when the public's opposed to them? There's only one
way. You have to have people reduce the significance of those issues. Maybe
they still oppose you on socioeconomic policies, but they don't care that
much 'cause there's something more important. The thing that's more
important is somebody's going to come and destroy you—and when somebody's going to come and destroy you, you forget everything else and you
trust the grand leader who may miraculously save us. Now that's the sce-
nario that was paraded right through the 80s, year after year, and we're seeing it again. So if you take a look at the . . . well, you've been following it.
. . . Up until September of last year, Saddam Hussein was portrayed as a ter-

rible guy. In September, he suddenly became an imminent threat to our survival. Now that's when Condoleezza Rice showed up with the mushroom
cloud in New York, and . . . every time Bush opens his mouth, [she] says,
"We gotta stop him now, or he's going to come after us." And that's unique
to the United States. That's the only country in the world where people not
only hate Saddam Hussein but fear him. Outside of Iraq, nobody fears him.
Like in Iran or Italy, you don't expect him to invade, you know. Here, people fear him and that's the way you whip people into . . . into support for
power and you can push through your domestic policies. Why September?
Well, you know, it's when the congressional mid-term elections begin.
They'd never have won the elections if there hadn't been this shift in popular attitudes. And then they're going to need another one. They can't go on
to the presidential election without having a victory over an awesome foe .
. . in their hands. And, of course, it will be portrayed . . . whatever happens,
it will be portrayed as a liberation. If it turns out to be a catastrophe, as it
might, that'll be Saddam Hussein's fault. But, in one way or another, it'll be
a wonderful liberation, just like Hitler's conquests were presented internal-
ly as liberating the oppressed population and so on and so forth. . . .

> *Of course the people don't want war. Why should some poor slob on a
> farm want to risk his life in a war when the best he can get out of it is to
> come back to his farm in one piece? Naturally the common people don't
> want war: neither in Russia, nor in England, nor for that matter in
> Germany. That is understood. But, after all, it is the leaders of the coun-
> try who determine the policy and it is always a simple matter to drag the
> people along, whether it is a democracy, or a fascist dictatorship, or a par-
> liament, or a communist dictatorship. Voice or no voice, the people can
> always be brought to the bidding of the leaders. That is easy. All you have
> to do is tell them they are being attacked, and denounce the peacemakers
> for lack of patriotism and exposing the country to danger. It works the
> same in any country.*
> —Hermann Göring, successor designate to Hitler, at the
> Nuremberg Trials, April 18, 1946

NOAM CHOMSKY: And what's the next one? Well, you know, a number of
choices, since it has to be much weaker, 'cause you don't want to confront
anyone else. It could be Syria, it could be Iran, except they're not so easy to
handle. It could be the Andean region. You know, there are a lot of possibilities for much weaker enemies that can be created as monsters to destroy
and then to proceed. . . . And, furthermore, they've made it . . . it's not like
they're being very secret about it. If you read the national strategy report of
last September, it's pretty brazen. It says, essentially: "We're going to rule the

world by force and . . . we're never going to permit a competitor to arise. So, if it looks like anyone, anywhere, is a potential competitor, we'll destroy them." And [the report] said it in those words—I mean, so clearly. . . . Right through the foreign policy elite in the United States, there's unprecedented opposition to this. I mean the foreign policy journalists; the institutions are writing articles which I've never seen before, saying, you know, "You're going off on a very dangerous course." Their criticisms are on very narrow grounds. They say it's going to harm the United States, but the criticisms are very strong and the administration pays no attention to them. It . . . knows they're right. It does not try to refute them. There's no point in telling the administration that what you're doing is likely to increase prolif-eration of weapons of mass destruction and terror—they know that. You know, so OK, they don't want terrorist acts in the United States, but if somebody blows up a hotel somewhere, that's OK, you know. You can use that to intensify discipline and control and push through your own agenda. Same with weapons of mass destruction. I mean, they're proliferating them and they know it, but we're going to have way more than anyone else so we'll just overwhelm the world by violence.

Actually, . . . what the US is teaching the world right at this minute is an extremely ugly lesson, and you have to kind of admire the discipline of intellectuals and media not to put it in headlines. I'm sure everyone out there understands it. Just take a look at North Korea and Iraq. I mean, what they're teaching the world is, "You want to protect yourself from us; you'd better have a deterrent, either weapons of mass destruction or a credible threat of terror. Otherwise, we'll smash you. If you're totally weak and com-pletely defenseless, and practically wiped out, yeah, then we'll attack you, like Iraq. But if you cause some trouble, we're not going to get close to you." I mean, . . . it doesn't take a genius to figure this out; it takes discipline for headline writers not to put headlines about it. But that's the lesson that's being taught the world and the Bush administration knows it, of course— they're not imbeciles—and they simply don't care because it will fit into their long-term agenda, if indeed there are threatening forces out there.

1989

VICTORIA DE GRAZIA: There was a lot of discussion just at the end of the 1980s about the capacity not just of the Soviet Union, but of the United States, to sustain its informal empire. The problem of the Soviet Union as an alternative economic political power ceased to exist. And the European Union, though starting to consolidate itself much more rapidly, was not seen as an alternative economic— much less political or military—regional power. So, [after] lots of worries [in] the 1980s, by the early 1990s it was seen that the United States had emerged as the winner. And not just the winner militarily, because the Soviet danger was no longer there, but somehow it was doing all sorts of right economically. And I think that if one goes and begins to look at the 1990s, it's a period where many, many possibilities for changing the American role in a very effective way were lost. First of all, it was thought that there would be a great peace dividend [now] that the US would also begin to disarm, [to] transform its way of doing military operations. And that had been looked for for a long time. And there was never that peace dividend. There was never that conversion to a different kind of military security stance.

XXI CENTURY

GORE VIDAL: Back in '39 our greatest historian, Charles A. Beard, wrote: "The destiny of Europe and Asia has not been committed, under God, to the keeping of the United States; and only conceit, dreams of grandeur, vain imaginings, lust for power, or a desire to escape from our domestic perils and obligations could possibly make us suppose that Providence has appointed us his chosen people for the pacification of the earth. Those Americans who refuse to plunge blindly into the maelstrom of European and Asiatic politics are not defeatist or neurotic. They are giving evidence of sanity, not cowardice, of adult thinking as distinguished from infantilism. They intend to preserve and defend the Republic. America is not to be Rome or Britain. It is to be America."

GEORGE W. BUSH (State of the Union speech, January 29, 2003): America is a strong nation, and honorable in the use of our strength. We exercise power without conquest, and we sacrifice for the liberty of strangers. Americans are a free people, who know that freedom is the right of every person and the future of every nation. The liberty we prize is not America's gift to the world, it is God's gift to humanity.

TIMOTHY MITCHELL: Well, the claim is often made that the US is somehow different from other great powers, other imperial powers, in that it exercises its international power in an ethical way or in a moral way and that somehow is different. All imperial powers have always claimed that for themselves, and it has always been a very misleading claim to make. The United States pursues its own national interests as defined by those who are in power in the US, and ethics are not a part of that calculation.

HOWARD ZINN: The United States has always, in its policy, been motivated by the desire to control other countries. It hasn't cared whether these countries are dictatorships or democracies. The one thing that it has cared about is, "Now, will this government do what we tell it to do," you know. During the Cold War, . . . the excuse was communism—you know, "We're opposed to this government because it's communist." But that didn't make any sense because the United States opposed governments that were not communist, as in Guatemala, in Chile. . . . Not communist, maybe slightly to the left. . . . These are governments that nationalized in Guatemala, the sugar fields, and [in] Chile, the copper companies, and so on. So, basically the United States wants to control whoever governs Iraq.

NOAM CHOMSKY: Of course, "empire" is a loose word; like, you know, the United States is not going to colonize Italy—it's not that kind of an empire. But in the sense of being able to be a hegemonic force which will determine the course of world affairs, punish those who don't go along, and tolerate those who do go along—if that's what an empire is, it's not even secret. I mean, when Bush and Powell and the rest of them go to the Security Council, they say it. You know, they say as clearly as they can: "You can go along with us. . . . Give us the authority we want and be relevant, or you can withhold that authority and we'll do it anyway and you'll be irrelevant. Powell, Bush, everyone else says it in those words. How can you not hear them? . . . You have to be obsessively deaf not to hear them. So, yeah, of course, they're telling us that as clear as they can. . . . In fact, the way they're trying to line people up for support of the war is just, you know, . . . I mean, it's being reported, but it's being reported without [an explanation of] what it means. Now what they're saying . . . what they're telling countries is, "You go along with us or you're going to be punished, and we have a lot of ways of punishing you. So, you go along with us 'cause we're strong and violent and repressive." That's what they're saying. And, "If you don't go along with us, you're going to feel it." And that's supposed to be a good thing. I mean, you know, we have examples like that in history. You don't have to look back very far.

> And as for a flag for the Philippine Province, it is easily managed. We can have a special one—our States do it: we can have just our usual flag, with the white stripes painted black and the stars replaced by the skull and cross-bones.
>
> —Mark Twain, "To the Person Sitting in Darkness,"
> North American Review, February 1901

Anti-war demonstration in Central Park, New York, October 6, 2002

APPENDIX

PROJECT FOR THE NEW AMERICAN CENTURY
STATEMENT OF PRINCIPLES

June 3, 1997

American foreign and defense policy is adrift. Conservatives have criticized the incoherent policies of the Clinton Administration. They have also resisted isolationist impulses from within their own ranks. But conservatives have not confidently advanced a strategic vision of America's role in the world. They have not set forth guiding principles for American foreign policy. They have allowed differences over tactics to obscure potential agreement on strategic objectives. And they have not fought for a defense budget that would maintain American security and advance American interests in the new century.

We aim to change this. We aim to make the case and rally support for American global leadership.

As the 20th century draws to a close, the United States stands as the world's preeminent power. Having led the West to victory in the Cold War, America faces an opportunity and a challenge: Does the United States have the vision to build upon the achievements of past decades? Does the

United States have the resolve to shape a new century favorable to American principles and interests?

We are in danger of squandering the opportunity and failing the challenge. We are living off the capital—both the military investments and the foreign policy achievements—built up by past administrations. Cuts in foreign affairs and defense spending, inattention to the tools of statecraft, and inconstant leadership are making it increasingly difficult to sustain American influence around the world. And the promise of short-term commercial benefits threatens to override strategic considerations. As a consequence, we are jeopardizing the nation's ability to meet present threats and to deal with potentially greater challenges that lie ahead.

We seem to have forgotten the essential elements of the Reagan Administration's success: a military that is strong and ready to meet both present and future challenges; a foreign policy that boldly and purposefully promotes American principles abroad; and national leadership that accepts the United States' global responsibilities.

Of course, the United States must be prudent in how it exercises its power. But we cannot safely avoid the responsibilities of global leadership or the costs that are associated with its exercise. America has a vital role in maintaining peace and security in Europe, Asia, and the Middle East. If we shirk our responsibilities, we invite challenges to our fundamental interests. The history of the 20th century should have taught us that it is important to shape circumstances before crises emerge, and to meet threats before they become dire. The history of this century should have taught us to embrace the cause of American leadership.

Our aim is to remind Americans of these lessons and to draw their consequences for today. Here are four consequences:

- we need to increase defense spending significantly if we are to carry out our global responsibilities today and modernize our armed forces for the future;
- we need to strengthen our ties to democratic allies and to challenge regimes hostile to our interests and values;
- we need to promote the cause of political and economic freedom abroad;
- we need to accept responsibility for America's unique role in preserving and extending an international order friendly to our security, our prosperity, and our principles.

Such a Reaganite policy of military strength and moral clarity may not be fashionable today. But it is necessary if the United States is to build on the successes of this past century and to ensure our security and our greatness in the next.

Elliott Abrams	*Donald Kagan*
Gary Bauer	*Zalmay Khalilzad*
William J. Bennett	*I. Lewis Libby*
Jeb Bush	*Norman Podhoretz*
Dick Cheney	*Dan Quayle*
Eliot A. Cohen	*Peter W. Rodman*
Midge Decter	*Stephen P. Rosen*
Paula Dobriansky	*Henry S. Rowen*
Steve Forbes	*Donald Rumsfeld*
Aaron Friedberg	*Vin Weber*
Francis Fukuyama	*George Weigel*
Frank Gaffney	*Paul Wolfowitz*
Fred C. Ikle	

PROJECT FOR THE NEW AMERICAN CENTURY

January 26, 1998

The Honorable William J. Clinton
President of the United States
Washington, DC

Dear Mr. President:

We are writing you because we are convinced that current American policy toward Iraq is not succeeding, and that we may soon face a threat in the Middle East more serious than any we have known since the end of the Cold War. In your upcoming State of the Union Address, you have an opportunity to chart a clear and determined course for meeting this threat. We urge you to seize that opportunity, and to enunciate a new strategy that would secure the interests of the U.S. and our friends and allies around the world. That strategy should aim, above all, at the removal of Saddam Hussein's regime from power. We stand ready to offer our full support in this difficult but necessary endeavor.

The policy of "containment" of Saddam Hussein has been steadily eroding over the past several months. As recent events have demonstrated, we can no longer depend on our partners in the Gulf War coalition to continue to uphold the sanctions or to punish Saddam when he blocks or evades UN inspections. Our ability to ensure that Saddam Hussein is not producing weapons of mass destruction, therefore, has substantially diminished. Even if full inspections were eventually to resume, which now seems highly unlikely, experience has shown that it is difficult if not impossible to monitor Iraq's chemical and biological weapons production. The lengthy period during which the inspectors will have been unable to enter many Iraqi facilities has made it even less likely that they will be able to uncover all of Saddam's secrets. As a result, in the not-too-distant future we will be unable to determine with any reasonable level of confidence whether Iraq does or does not possess such weapons.

Such uncertainty will, by itself, have a seriously destabilizing effect on the entire Middle East. It hardly needs to be added that if Saddam does acquire the capability to deliver weapons of mass destruction, as he is almost certain to do if we continue along the present course, the safety of American troops in the region, of our friends and allies like Israel and the moderate Arab states, and a significant portion of the world's supply of oil will all be put at hazard. As you have rightly declared, Mr. President, the security of the world in the first part of the 21st century will be determined largely by how we handle this threat.

Given the magnitude of the threat, the current policy, which depends for its success upon the steadfastness of our coalition partners and upon the cooperation of Saddam Hussein, is dangerously inadequate. The only acceptable strategy is one that eliminates the possibility that Iraq will be able to use or threaten to use weapons of mass destruction. In the near term, this means a willingness to undertake military action as diplomacy is clearly failing. In the long term, it means removing Saddam Hussein and his regime from power. That now needs to become the aim of American foreign policy.

We urge you to articulate this aim, and to turn your Administration's attention to implementing a strategy for removing Saddam's regime from power. This will require a full complement of diplomatic, political and military efforts. Although we are fully aware of the dangers and difficulties in implementing this policy, we believe the dangers of failing to do so are far greater. We believe the U.S. has the authority under existing UN resolutions to take the necessary steps, including military steps, to protect our vital interests in the Gulf. In any case, American policy cannot continue to be crippled by a misguided insistence on unanimity in the UN Security Council.

We urge you to act decisively. If you act now to end the threat of weapons of mass destruction against the U.S. or its allies, you will be acting in the most fundamental national security interests of the country. If we accept a course of weakness and drift, we put our interests and our future at risk.

Sincerely,

Elliott Abrams	*William Kristol*
Richard L. Armitage	*Richard Perle*
William J. Bennett	*Peter W. Rodman*
Jeffrey Bergner	*Donald Rumsfeld*
John Bolton	*William Schneider, Jr.*
Paula Dobriansky	*Vin Weber*
Francis Fukuyama	*Paul Wolfowitz*
Robert Kagan	*R. James Woolsey*
Zalmay Khalilzad	*Robert B. Zoellick*

Credits

XXI Century, an award-winning series of seven one-hour documentaries by Gabriele Zamparini and Lorenzo Meccoli, is available in a two-DVD set from Bullfrog Films, P.O. Box 149, Oley, PA 19547, (800) 543-3764, www.bullfrogfilms.com. To know more about the documentary and the book, please visit www.TheCatsDream.com, where you'll also find a list of people and organizations devoted to peace, freedom, and social justice.

XXI Century
a documentary film in seven parts
written and directed by
Gabriele Zamparini

produced by
Lorenzo Meccoli and Gabriele Zamparini

associate producer
Benson Gilchrist

editor
Lorenzo Meccoli

with
Joshua Berger
and
Kevin Brooks
Sandra Nash
Morgan Neville
Hilary Peabody

assistant editor
Vijay Ramachandran
Yvette Shin
Jan-Luc VanDamme

sound editor
Grundik Kasyansky

colorist
Andrew Carranza

production assistant
Angela Gianforcaro

camera, lighting and sound
Lorenzo Meccoli
Gabriele Zamparini

Washington, DC October 26 unit:
camera—Shawn Bell
camera—Alex Stikich
assistant camera—Brooke Dodson-Lavelle
assistant camera—Benson Gilchrist
interviewer—Stephanie Daddi
interviewer—Laetitia Lemaitre

Washington, DC January 18 unit:
camera—Lorenzo Meccoli
camera—Gabriele Zamparini
assistant camera—Claudia Bertonati
assistant camera—Benson Gilchrist
assistant camera—Jan-Luc VanDamme

New York City February 15 unit:
camera—Lorenzo Meccoli
camera—Gabriele Zamparini
assistant camera—Benson Gilchrist
assistant camera—Vijay Ramachandran

additional footage from:
ITN Archive
George Bush Presidential Library and Museum
Ronald Reagan Presidential Library
Lyndon Baines Johnson Presidential Library and Museum

Truman Presidential Museum and Library
Franklin D. Roosevelt Presidential Library and Museum
U.S. Department of Defense
U.S. Federal Bureau of Investigation
U.S. National Archives and Records Administration
U.S. State Department
The White House Web Site
Collection, The Supreme Court Historical Society
Richard Strauss, Smithsonian Institution

special thanks to:
Amy Goodman and Democracy Now!
for the interview of Gore Vidal

The Nation Institute
for the Gore Vidal event at the New York Society for Ethical Culture

International Physicians
for the Prevention of Nuclear War
for photos and videos on the effects of the first Gulf War
and of the UN sanctions on Iraqi civilians

Emergency for the photos of its hospitals
in Sierra Leone, Cambodia, Afghanistan, Iraq

New York City Independent Media Center
for the poster "a threat to peace"

Danny Schechter for the documentary
"Counting on Democracy"

September Eleventh Families for Peaceful Tomorrows
for the videos of their travels to Afghanistan and Iraq

Applied Research Institute of Jerusalem for the photos
of the Occupied Palestinian Territories

Fondation Arabe pour l'Image
Collections Badran Abdel Razzak,
Latif el Ani, Eid Barakat, Hanna Halaby, Aimée Kettaneh,
Sami Khoury, Nada Zeineh.
© Fondation Arabe pour l'Image

Sister Arlene Flaherty and the
Intercommunity Center for Justice and Peace
for their photographs of Iraqi people

Arab Film Distribution for the footage from:
"Jenin Jenin" by Mohammad Bakri
"Gaza Strip" by James Longley

special thanks for their photographs to:
Fred Askew
Eric Bertuccio
Nathan Blaney
Steffie Kinglake
James Longley
Michael Muench

special thanks for their help to:
Ketty Agnesani · Zainab Bahrani · Gabriela Bulisova
Alberto Colombi · David Cline · Uri Gal-Ed
Amy Goodman · Taya Grobow · Jad Isaac
Janine Jaquet · Joyce Katzberg · Colleen Kelly
James Longley · Mark Majzner · Lynn Martin
Timothy Mitchell · The Nation Institute · Ana Nogueira
Raed E Abed Rabbo · Lucien Samaha
Tamara Sawaya · Danny Schechter · Dread Scott
John Sinno · Bev Stohl · Jeanne Strole
Claudia Wunschmann · Akram Zaatari

MUSIC

"Is It For Freedom?"
Written and Performed by Sara Thomsen
copyright 1999 Sara Thomsen
Courtesy of Sara Thomsen

"By Breath"
Written and Performed by Sara Thomsen
copyright 2003 Sara Thomsen
Courtesy of Sara Thomsen

"Keepin' the Peace"
Written and Performed by Sara Thomsen
copyright 2003 Sara Thomsen
Courtesy of Sara Thomsen

"Freedom Song"
Written and Performed by Sara Thomsen
copyright 2003 Sara Thomsen
Courtesy of Sara Thomsen

"3M's"
Written by Mike Dailey, Cornel West,
Clifton West, Derek D.O.A. Allen
Performed by Cornel West
copyright 2001 Sheridan Square Entertainment, LLC.
Courtesy of 4BMWMB, Inc.

"Frontline (Interlude)"
Written by Mike Dailey, Cornel West, Kelly Keyes
Performed by Cornel West
copyright 2001 Sheridan Square Entertainment, LLC.
Courtesy of 4BMWMB, Inc.

"The Finale"
Written by Cornel West and Derek D.O.A. Allen
Performed by Cornel West
copyright 2001 Sheridan Square Entertainment, LLC.
Courtesy of 4BMWMB, Inc.

"The Second Baghdad" (Baghdad AlThania)
Written and Performed by Rahim AlHaj
copyright 2002 Rahim AlHaj
Courtesy of Rahim AlHaj

"Missing" (Showak)
Written and Performed by Rahim AlHaj
copyright 2002 Rahim AlHaj
Courtesy of Rahim AlHaj

"Horses" (Khaiyul)
Written and Performed by Rahim AlHaj
copyright 2002 Rahim AlHaj
Courtesy of Rahim AlHaj

"Amen"
Written and Performed by Pamela Means
copyright 2003 Pamela Means
Courtesy of Pamela Means

"Her Eyes"
Written and Performed by Jim Page
copyright 2002 Jim Page, Whid-Isle Music, BMI
Courtesy of Jim Page, Whid-Isle Music, BMI

"In Search of Love (Silent Are The Tears)"
Written and Performed by Onaje Allan Gumbs
copyright 2003 Onaje Music Publishing ASCAP
Courtesy of Onaje Music Publishing ASCAP

"Remember Their Innocence"
Written and Performed by Onaje Allan Gumbs
copyright 2003 Onaje Music Publishing ASCAP
Courtesy of Onaje Music Publishing ASCAP

"Yellow Cab Fever"
Written and Performed by Onaje Allan Gumbs
copyright 2003 Onaje Music Publishing ASCAP
Courtesy of Onaje Music Publishing ASCAP

"Conversations"
Written and Performed by Onaje Allan Gumbs
copyright 2003 Onaje Music Publishing ASCAP
Courtesy of Onaje Music Publishing ASCAP

The following music is courtesy of NAXOS

Tomaso Albinoni
Adagio in G minor (Arranged Giazzotto)
Capella Istropolitana—Richard Edlinger

J. S. Bach—Gounod
Ave Maria
Ingrid Kertesi, Soprano
Camerata Budapest—László Kovács

J. S. Bach
Suite No. 3 in D major, BWV 1068-Aria
Capella Istropolitana—Jaroslav Dvorák

J. S. Bach
Concerto in C minor, BWV1060
Emilia Csánky, Oboe / Béla Bánfalvi, Violin

J. S. Bach
Goldberg Variations, BWV 988-Aria
Chen Pi-Hsien, Piano

Wolfgang Amadeus Mozart
Requiem (Complited by Franz Xaver Süssmayr)
Magdeléna Hajóssyová, Soprano / Jaroslava Horská, Alto / Jozef Kundlák, Tenor / Peter Mikulás, Bass

Wolfgang Amadeus Mozart
Exsultate, jubilate, K 165
Anna di Mauro, Mezzo-Soprano / Priti Coles, Soprano
Kosice Teachers' Choir
Camerata Cassovia / Johannes Wildner

Camille Saint-Saëns
Carnaval des Animaux
Marian Lapsansky—Peter Toperczer, Piano
Czecho-Slovak Radio Symphony Orchestra
Ondrej Lenárd

Erik Satie
Trois Gymnopédies (Piano Version)
Klára Körmendi, Piano

Erik Satie
Trois Gymnopédies (Orchestra Version)
Orchestre Symphonique et Lyrique de Nancy
Jérôme Kaltenbach

Erik Satie
Six Gnossiennes
Klára Körmendi, Piano

Erik Satie
Je te veux (Valse pour piano)
Klára Körmendi, Piano

Francis Scott Key
Star Spangled Banner
Slovak Radio Symphony Orchestra (Bratislava)
Peter Breiner

Richard Strauss
Also Sprach Zarathustra Op. 30
Slovak Philharmonic—Zdenek Kosler

Johann Strauss II
Blue Danube Waltz, Op. 314
Strauss Festival Orchestra—Ondrej Lenárd

For Product Safety Concerns and Information please contact our EU
representative GPSR@taylorandfrancis.com
Taylor & Francis Verlag GmbH, Kaufingerstraße 24, 80331 München, Germany

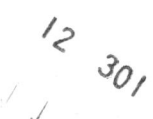